SUNDERLAND HARBOUR IN 1800.

HISTORY OF SUNDERLAND

BY
WILLIAM CRANMER MITCHELL

Author of
"*History of St. John's Masonic Lodge, No. 80, Sunderland.*"

WITH A FOREWORD BY
SAMUEL HOOLE, M.A.,
PRINCIPAL OF THE SUNDERLAND DAY TRAINING COLLEGE.

ILLUSTRATED

E. J. MORTEN (Publishers)
Didsbury, Manchester, England.

First Printed 1919
THE HILLS PRESS LTD.
Holmside, Sunderland

Republished 1972
E. J. MORTEN (Publishers)/E & L Ass.
10 Warburton Street, Didsbury,
Manchester, England

ISBN 0 901598 53 4

Printed in Great Britain by
Scolar Press Limited, Menston, Yorkshire

FOREWORD.

This is primarily a book for school use but it will, I am sure, appeal to the wider public of the town and be read with interest and valued as a concise and interesting record.

To the child, stories of deeds speak for themselves, and every deed of heroism, of benevolence, of patriotism, is a concrete embodiment of a precious virtue. The author seems to have kept this well in mind throughout his account of the rise and growth of Sunderland, and his interesting records of many of its famous men and women.

The book also shows that commerce produces its heroes no less than war. Doubtless the same qualities which made the Havelocks famous as soldiers were exemplified by the father as a shipbuilder. Courage, resource, industry, integrity, are surely no less notable when applied to commerce than in other spheres.

And the record in this local history of industrial and commercial venture is surely not without its inspiration. To the story of noble achievements, which is the story of Sunderland, the founders and captains of industry, the sailors, the keelmen, the colliers, all contribute equally with the soldiers, the scholars, the artists, and the philanthropists. It is a story of absorbing interest, and cannot fail to awaken and stimulate the growth of a genuine local patriotism, from which the wider patriotism of Country and Empire may spring.

To one who has not the privilege of claiming Sunderland as a birthplace, there is, after reading this little book, an added pride in being a Sunderlander by adoption. In one who is a native of the town, how much stronger must be the feeling, and, if this feeling can be implanted and cultivated in the breasts of the children of the town, as I am sure it can, and as I believe the author aims to do, it might well be a great gain.

S.H.

PREFACE.

The first history of Sunderland was published one hundred years ago, by Mr. James Garbutt. The work was well illustrated and contained the names of the subscribers to whom the book was sold for one guinea. In 1830, Mr. James Burnett's history was published. Mr. J. W. Summers' history was printed in serial form in 1858, but the work was never completed as the author was overtaken by blindness and so unfortunately unable to complete his researches. In 1892 appeared the history of our town by Mr. Taylor Potts. These four local histories are all out of print and rarely to be bought. The *early* history of Sunderland is recorded best by Garbutt and Summers, while the works of Burnett and Potts relate principally to the condition and progress of the town during the lifetime of the authors. The four works are of great value to students of local history.

My object in writing the present history of Sunderland and District is to contribute some assistance towards the study of local history in the senior schools and colleges of my native town, and to provide a useful book for Sunderland people who take more than a passing interest in the history and prosperity of our ancient town.

An educational expert has written about this history :—

> "It fully meets an educational need in the Elementary and Secondary schools of Sunderland. It supplies suitable information for the sustenance and development of the growing mind as well as matter, hints and suggestions, for reflection and action by mature ones. The work not only forms an introduction to the study of national history but is itself the natural history 'in little' for this history of Sunderland is in miniature, the story of the evolution of the nation. The book is an excellent and valuable addition to local history."

I take this opportunity of expressing my thanks to Mr. J. A. Charlton Deas for permission to use information in the Library Circulars ; to Mr. J. T. Hindmarch for his valuable assistance ; to Mr. John Robinson for the use of his local historical publications and to the Manager of the Cambridge University Press for granting permission to use a few extracts from the recently published book on the Geography of Durham.

1919.   W.C.M.

CONTENTS.

CHAPTER I.

PRE-HISTORIC TIMES.—Approximate dates of pre-historic ages; Palæolithic age; Neolithic age; Bronze age; Celtic age; Pre-historic stone circles; Pre-historic pottery; Local British barrows; Pre-historic remains in Sunderland Museum.

CHAPTER II.

ROMAN PERIOD.—Military roads and stations in Durham; Roman remains in Sunderland and district; Roman altars found in Weardale; Roman remains in Black Gate Museum, Newcastle; Ancient Britons under Roman Rule.

CHAPTER III.

SAXON & DANISH TIMES.—Saxon Kingdom of Northumbria; The Abbot Biscop and the Priest Bede; Monasteries at Monkwearmouth and Jarrow; Danish Incursions and Settlement; Athelstan's gift to the Church; Bishopwearmouth in Saxon Times.

CHAPTER IV.

NORMAN & PLANTAGENET PERIODS.—The Normans invade Durham; How the land was held in Norman times; The Hilton Family; Bishop Pudsey's Charter 1154; Boldon Book 1180; Charter granted by Henry III, 1274; Sunderland in Plantagenet Times.

CHAPTER V.

TUDOR & STUART TIMES.—Queen Elizabeth's Commission of 1558; Bishop Morton's Charter 1634; The Cival War; Tragedy on the Town Moor; Tragedy at Bishopwearmouth; The old Rectory; Oaths of Supremacy and Obedience taken by Sunderland people; The first Pier 1699; Sir Ambrose Crowley; Social Condition in Sunderland during the 17th Century.

CHAPTER VI.

HANOVERIAN PERIOD (Part I).—Pier, Lighthouses, and Docks; Trade of the Port; Sunderland Life-boats; The Three Bridges; Sunderland Parish Church; The Town Moor; Forts and Spa Well; Sunderland as a Seaside Resort; Population and Growth of Sunderland; High Street and Wearmouth Walk; Street Names; Hendon and Hendon Dene; Hendon old Mill.

CHAPTER VII.

HANOVERIAN PERIOD (Part II).—Sunderland in the time of George III; Principal Streets; The Market; Watchmen; Water Supply; Coaches and Sedan Chairs; Ballast Hills; Illustrious Visitors.

CHAPTER VIII.

ANCIENT CUSTOMS, SPORTS, & PUNISHMENTS.—Perambulating the Boundaries ; St. Crispin's Day and Cloy's Day ; How Naval Victories were announced ; Cock Fighting ; Bull Baiting ; Fox Hunting ; Horse Racing on the Moor ; Bowling on the Moor; Riding the Stang ; The Cage, Stocks and Pillory.

CHAPTER IX.

THE RIVER WEAR.—Towns, Castles, and Ancient Churches on the Wear.

CHAPTER X.

SHIPBUILDERS & SHIPBUILDING.—Early History ; Wooden Ships ; Famous Sunderland Vessels ; The Shipwrights ; The Sixteen Local Shipbuilders ; Number of Vessels Launched.

CHAPTER XI.

THE COAL TRADE.—Early History ; Amount exported ; The Colliers and their Crews ; Keels and Keelmen.

CHAPTER XII.

THE POTTERIES.—Early History ; Roman Pottery ; Local Potteries of the 18th and 19th Centuries ; Work in the Potteries ; The decline of Local Potteries ; Pottery in the Local Museum.

CHAPTER XIII.

SUNDERLAND GLASS TRADE.—Early History ; Wear Glass Works ; The Great Exhibition of 1851 ; Decline of Local Glass Trade ; Exports of Bottles and Glass.

CHAPTER XIV.

OTHER INDUSTRIES.—Marine Engines ; Paper Making ; The Lime Trade ; Local Trades of the Past ; Salmon and Whale Fisheries ; Furriers ; Iron Trade ; Grindstones ; Salt, etc.

CHAPTER XV.

MEN & WOMEN OF WHOM SUNDERLAND IS PROUD.—Bede and Biscop ; The Heroic Havelocks ; Brave Sunderland Sailors, Jack Crawford, Captain Hornsby, Joseph Hodgson, Harry Watts, Captain Rackley ; Doctor Clanny ; William Shield ; Local Artists, Authors and Actors, Lieutenant George Maling, V.C. ; Dame Dorothy Williamson ; Mrs. Jane Gibson ; Mrs. Elizabeth Donnison ; Mrs. Woodcock ; The Sunderland Florence Nightingale ; The Sunderland Grace Darling.

CHAPTER XVI.

SUNDERLAND IN 1918.—Trade ; Public Buildings ; Town Hall ; Library, Museum and Art Gallery ; Infirmaries ; Technical College ; Training College ; Victoria Hall ; New Police Buildings ; Philanthropic Institutions ; Orphan Asylum and War Record ; The Grange School ; Teachers War Record ; The Parks ; Roker.

CHAPTER XVII.

GREATER SUNDERLAND.—Southwick ; Castletown ; North Hylton ; Biddick ; Ford or South Hylton ; Fulwell ; Cleadon ; Whitburn ; Boldon ; Offerton ; Cox Green ; Grangetown ; Tunstall ; Silksworth ; Ryhope ; Seaham ; Burdon ; Herrington ; Newbottle ; Sunderland War Records ; Events of Local Interest.

ILLUSTRATIONS.

		Page
SUNDERLAND HARBOUR IN 1800		FRONTIS.
MONKWEARMOUTH CHURCH PRIOR TO 1874	- -	25
BISHOPWEARMOUTH IN 1810	- -	38
BISHOPWEARMOUTH RECTORY IN 1807	- -	53
SUNDERLAND CHURCH IN 1719	- -	70
WEARMOUTH BRIDGE IN 1796	- -	98
HYLTON CASTLE IN 1746	- -	106
THE GRANGE, BISHOPWEARMOUTH, IN 1789	- -	122

HISTORY OF SUNDERLAND

CHAPTER I.

Pre-   AT some time or other we must all have felt
Historic curious as to what our district was like in
Times   remote ages, and what kind of people once
lived where we now dwell; but it is only during the past fifty years that Archæologists have made successful and systematic attempts to pierce the darkness which preceded the long dawn of history thus enabling us to have interesting peeps into those far distant times. By the combined efforts of Archæologists and Geologists it has been possible to fix the following as the approximate dates of the four pre-historic ages of our district through which man passed before the period of written history:—

1. Palæolithic or Old Stone Age..B.C. 250,000 to 60,000
2. Neolithic or New Stone Age...B.C. 60,000 to 2,000.
3. Bronze Age ......................B.C. 2,000 to 500.
4. Early Iron or Late Celtic Age..B.C. 500 to A.D. 45.

These periods were not uniform and contemporary throughout Britain and there was no sudden change from one to another so they may be considered as stages in human progress rather than as periods of time.

The   THE earliest known evidence of the existence
Palaeoli- of man in Britain is of a time when this Coun-
thic Age try was joined to the continent of Europe and
had a cold climate with the appropriate fauna, including the mammoth and other animals now extinct. These first inhabitants are now spoken of as the men of

the Palæolithic or old Stone age. From the examination of their skeletons found in old clay pits, ancient river beds, and caverns we learn that they were a stunted race, with large heads, low foreheads, large and strong jaws, broad, deep chests, and short curved legs. They lived by hunting and fishing and also used roots and berries as food. So far as we know, all races of mankind have passed through a state of civilization during which the use of metals was unknown. This we call the stone age, as stone implements were used for many purposes during this period. The weapons in use during this old stone age were made of rudely shaped flints brought into shape by percussion and flaking. They were rough and unpolished and without handles of any kind. No remains of the Palæolithic Age have been found in the county of Durham, whose climate it is supposed then resembled that of the Arctic regions.

The Neolithic Age THE men of the Neolithic or new Stone Age succeeded the former long ages later, when our country had been separated from the continent though both climate and configuration of the land were still different from what they are at the present day. They crossed the water, which separated Britain from the Continent, in primitive boats and on rafts, and took possession of the land, the older inhabitants being driven away or made slaves. They were taller and stronger than their predecessors and had reached a higher degree of culture. Their stone weapons were sharpened and polished with great skill and provided with handles. Their flint arrowheads were secured to the wood shafts by narrow strips of hide, put on raw and then dried in the sun. This resulted in a shrinkage which bound the head and shaft firmly together. They had acquired many domestic arts such as making pottery, cultivating the land, and had domesticated sheep, goats, pigs and dogs.

During the Neolithic Age the people buried their dead in *long* barrows or graves. Sometimes the body was cremated and the ashes placed in a clay vessel, now known as a Cinerary Urn, before burial; on other occasions the dead were buried wrapped in skins of animals. It is not certain which method was first generally in use. The Neolithic men spread as far as the extreme north of Scotland and all over the Hebridean Islands. There are many places in Weardale which local tradition assigns as the sites of ancient camps or towns of the Neolithic Age. The most remarkable is called the "Castles" and is situated near Wolsingham. This camp occupies about one acre of ground and is surrounded by a continuous heap of loose water-worn stones. It is in the form of a square, with an opening at one side. Within this enclosure would be constructed the huts of the people. Sites of other Pre-historic camps are situated at Eastgate, Shipley and Hamsterley.

The Bronze Age NEARLY four thousand years ago the men of the Neolithic Age were in their turn defeated by a superior race who also crossed from the continent.

These men of the Bronze Age were dark-haired and strong. They could spin wool and flax into thread to make cloth and they grew corn and ground it between two stones. Mixed with the flour thus obtained were particles of stone grit, and thus we find the teeth obtained from the burial places of the Bronze Age people to be much worn at the crown. They knew how to make bronze weapons and implements, though stone still continued to be used for many purposes. The introduction of the use of metals marks one of the most important steps in human progress. It is probable that copper was the first metal employed for making weapons until it was found that bronze, a metal composed of an alloy of copper and tin, was more durable. Many interesting relics of the Bronze Age have been found near Stanhope on the River Wear. In the year 1812 a hoard of bronze weapons and implements was found under some large rough stones. There were five spearheads, parts of a sword and breastplate, several tools resembling chisels, and a number of socketed axes.

Frequent discoveries were made between the years 1859 and 1872 in the Heathery Burn cave, one mile from Stanhope. This cave, which has now been quarried away by the Weardale Iron Company, was evidently the dwelling place of a community during the Bronze Age and the objects found included armlets, and rings of gold ; two swords, eight spearheads, three knives, nineteen tools, fourteen rings, fifteen pins and three armlets, all of bronze. Skeletons of men, women and children, together with articles of pottery, bones of sheep, and heaps of mussel, cockle and limpet shells were also found in the cave. Local discoveries of bronze ornaments found in our district include a bronze sword brought up from the bed of the Wear in 1855 by one of the River Wear Commissioners' dredgers.

During the Spring of 1878 there were found in one of the sea-worn caves at Whitburn many bones and other remains of primitive man. Five human skulls, bones of the red deer, the roe deer, the badger, and the marten were identified, and, most interesting of all, the skeleton of the Great Auk, an extinct sea-bird, the flesh of which had so long ago furnished a meal for these long vanished cave dwellers. The people of the Bronze Age buried their dead in *round* barrows, both after cremation and by inhumation; cinerary urns, drinking cups, food vessels and other pottery being usually placed in the graves. During this period our district was covered by large forests and swamps. Wolves, bears, boars, and beavers were common. The only part of our county which has not changed since that remote age is the dark, sweeping, heather-clad, moorland of the West.

The Celtic Age LAST of the pre-historic people came the Celts, nearly 2,500 years ago, in three successive swarms; first the Gaels, then the Britons, and much later the Belgae. They conquered the country and called it Britain. They were tall, strong people, with fair hair and blue eyes and they had weapons of iron. They were skilled workers in iron, bronze, wood and clay. These people attained a very considerable degree of civilization, so far as the conveniences and even the luxuries of life were concerned. They possessed a coinage stamped with regular dies and used various implements, the manufacture of which indicated a condition far in advance of barbarism. The materials of which their warlike and industrial implements were formed consisted of stone, bronze and iron. It has been thought that these may indicate three successive periods, but there is no indisputable reason for assigning them to different ages, as they may possibly vary only according to the social condition or degree of importance of the person or tribe to which they belonged. It is by no means certain that the barrows where stone implements have been found belong to an earlier time than those containing articles of bronze.

Several relics of this period have been found at Sunderland. There is a beautifully made stone axe hammer in the Newcastle Museum, which was found in the Wear just above the Sunderland Bridge and another of a larger size, perforated for a handle, was found at Millfield. Two stone hand querns, for grinding corn, were recently found, one near Bishopwearmouth Church and the other at Seaham. The Celtic people were famous for their wicker work, and their light and elegant baskets, adapted for all kinds of purposes, were highly prized in Rome. Their "coracles" or river boats were woven of compact and tenacious withes, and the walls of their huts were often composed of hurdles covered with an impenetrable coating of a kind of cement or plaster. We must remember, however, that the tribes living in our district, the "Brigantes," were less skilful than those of the South of England.

Pre-Historic Stone Circles THE ordinary school History of England contains information about some of the ancient British Leaders, i.e., the Druids, Cassivelaunus and Queen Boadicea but little is recorded about the great circles of stone like Stonehenge. This is the most famous pre-historic monument in the world. It is a circular group of huge stones, of which several have fallen or been destroyed in historic times. The probable date of erection is between 2000 and 1000 B.C. It may have been a temple of worship of the sun or for the honour of the great dead—an ancient British Westminster Abbey.

When some of the immense stones which had fallen

were raised in 1901 a number of stone tools and human bones were found.

Mr. C. H. E. Chubb of Bemerton Lodge, Salisbury, who bought Stonehenge in 1895 for £6600, presented it to the Nation in October 1918.

There are relics of some 200 other circles of similar but smaller stones in Great Britain. One is known to have stood near Eggleston in our County until the year 1809. This Druid circle is thus described on page 235 (Vol. 3) of Hutchinson's History of Durham (published in 1795) :—

"A mile to the north of the village of Eggleston stands an ancient monument, called the Standing Stone. It has consisted of an uniform circle of rough stones with an inward trench, and in the centre a cairn ; much of the material has been taken away to repair the roads."

The engraving in Hutchinson's History shows that the Durham stone circle was similar to the one still standing near Penrith and which is known in the neighbourhood as "Long Meg and her daughters."

In 1809 the large upright stones forming the circle were broken up and used for the inclosing walls then being built on the estate; probably the remainder of the internal cairn was then carried off to repair the adjoining roads.

It is recorded in the Saxon Chronicles of 891 and 1066 that a battle was fought in the year 603 between Ethelfrith, King of Northumbria, and Adan, King of the Scots, who resided at a place named "Egesan-stane."

The place of battle has been identified with Eggleston, in Durham, which from remote times had a noted circle of stones and a large archaic stone from which the village is said to derive its name.

Pre-Historic Pottery. BEFORE describing the local burial places of the ancient Britons, it is necessary to give a few particulars of pre-historic pottery, as a knowledge of this subject is of great value in dating objects found associated with it in British barrows.

The pottery of the Stone and Bronze Ages was made with local clays and fashioned by hand without the aid of the potter's wheel. The pottery thus made was frequently decorated with lines or borders by impressing a twisted cord or thong upon the substance of soft clay. Sometimes there were also zig-zag lines and combinations of straight lines apparently scratched with a pointed stick. Although pre-historic pottery is usually spoken of as "sun-dried" there can be no doubt that it was always fired, however imperfectly, in an open fire. Four kinds of pottery have been found in local barrows :—

1. Drinking cups or beakers. These are flat-based, decorated vessels with rather thin sides. They were made during the transition from the Stone Age to the early Bronze Age, and were used for liquid and perhaps also for solid food. They are usually from 5 to 10 inches in height, and though frequently found in pre-historic burial places in the North of England are very rarely found in the South.

2. Food vessels are usually basin-shaped and well decorated. They succeeded the drinking cups but are coarser, considerably thicker, and sometimes provided with lids or covers. They are of various shapes and from five to eight inches high.

3. The Cinerary urns are yet a later type of this pottery and were only used for cremated human

remains. They are the largest type of pottery, of many different shapes, and usually from 12 to 16 inches high, about 13 inches across the top, and 5 inches wide at the bottom.

4. Incense cups vary in shape and size, being from 3 to 4 inches high and from 2 to 4 inches in diameter. They are highly ornamented, and generally pierced round the sides in one or more places, as if to assist combustion. Some have lids, and others are frequently provided with loops as if for suspension. They are often found with cinerary urns and sometimes placed within them. Though found in Great Britain and Ireland, they have never been found in pre-historic graves on the Continent. Domestic vessels of clay, made during this period, are perfectly plain, and in no way resemble the sepulchral vessels described above.

Local Pre- Historic Remains
PRE-HISTORIC remains have been found at or near the summits of all the hills in our district. These barrows or ancient burial places are supposed to have been made for the remains of the distinguished chieftains or leaders who, in past ages, dwelt near the Wear.

The first pre-historic grave of which we have any local record was discovered on Humbledon Hill on the 7th September, 1750. In 1873, during the course of excavating for a reservoir on the top of this hill, two ancient British vases were found in an inverted position filled with bones that had been subjected to fire. Near these cinerary urns were discovered two skeletons of a great size, and also a short iron knife with a curved handle.

The late Canon Greenwell* was of opinion that the larger vase was of an exceedingly rare kind, which, as far as he knew, had only been found in one other part of England. Whether the urns and their contents were coeval with the skeletons he could not say, neither could it be certain who the depositors were.

It is recorded in Surtees' *History of the County of Durham* that a pre-historic grave was found on the southern peak of Tunstall Hill, in the year 1814. The rude sepulchre was formed of slabs of common limestone and covered with the same materials. In the cist were three ancient urns containing a rich dark mould in which were interspersed fragments of bone and some human teeth. These cinerary urns were supposed to belong to the Bronze Age. On the same hill another grave was accidentally discovered in 1887, whilst preparing the ground for a bonfire to commemorate the 50th anniversary of Queen Victoria's reign. The grave had been hewn out of the solid limestone and contained a human skeleton apparently of the Stone Age.

Similar pre-historic barrows have been discovered on Boyldon Hill in Mowbray Park, Steeple or Sand Hill, Hasting Hill, and on the hills near Southwick and Fulwell.

Warden Law, about five miles south west of our town has an interesting history. It is 646 feet high, the highest peak on the east coast of Durham. During Celtic times it was known as Weredun, *i.e.*, the hill of the Were (Wear). It is supposed to have been a meet-

* The Rev. Dr. Wm. Greenwell, the famous Archæologist, died at Durham on the 27th January, 1918, aged 97 years. He was an authority on all that pertained to the Ancient Britons and the Bronze Age. In his researches he had the assistance at one time of eminent investigators like the late Lord Avebury and Sir John Evans, and was associated with Professor Huxley.

ing place for both Saxons and Danes, and for ages a beacon fire was kept near the summit ready to be lighted when one of the frequent incursions of the Scots troubled the district. This hill was once covered to its summit with immense oak trees. It is mentioned in Fordyce's History of Durham that in July, 1822, when the Hetton Colliery Company were excavating to make a reservoir for water at the top of the hill, several large oak trees were discovered at a depth of from ten to twenty feet below the surface. One tree, measured by the workmen, was found to be 70 feet long, three feet in diameter at one end and two feet at the other. Pre-historic burials have taken place on this hill, and it is famous as one of the spots on which the bones of St. Cuthbert rested in the year 996 on their way from Ripon to the city of Durham.

Sand Hill and Hasting Hill are about two miles west of Sunderland, and on the summit of each important barrows have been examined. In February, 1876, the grave on Sand Hill was opened. This ancient grave was four feet long and two and a half feet wide, and was constructed of seven large flat stones; four large whinstone boulders formed the sides, the two end stones and the top or cover stone were limestone. In it was the skeleton of a man, past middle age, with two sepulchral food vessels near the head.

Remarkable skill and care were displayed when the ancient barrow on Hasting Hill was excavated in November, 1911, by Mr. C. T. Trechmann, B.Sc. The barrow, a round example. about 35 feet in diameter, probably belongs to the transitional period from the Neolithic Age to the early Bronze Age, considered to be about 4000 years ago. It contained both burnt and unburnt burials. All the pottery found was, of course, hand made, the potter's wheel not been used in Britain until the early Iron Age, commencing 500 B.C. The larger cist or grave was the primary burial of the barrow and that over which the mound of earth was erected, all the rest were secondary interments, let in after the mound was constructed.

It was sunk to a depth of 1½ feet in the solid limestone at the hilltop, lined with slabs of sandstone and magnesian limestone, and covered with a large slab of sandstone. The grave lay east and west, and contained the skeleton of a man about fifty years of age. The body lay on its right side facing south, the head to the west, the hands in front of the face, and the legs doubled up in a contracted position, usual in British barrows.

There were evidences of a greenstick fracture (that is, fracture in childhood) on one of the ribs; and traces of rheumatism in some of the joints. The objects accompanying the remains consisted of a vessel of the drinking cup type (which presumably had contained food) placed near the face, a rough flint knife in front of the body, and a bone pin behind the shoulder. The pin may have fastened some garment, or have fallen out of the hair. Remains of food also occurred in the cist, viz., burnt animal bones, unburnt fish bones, bird bones, and periwinkle shells.

A second cist made of four slabs of limestone with coverstones over the top was found in the N.E. edge of the barrow. This contained the skeleton of a child under 18 months old, which lay upon its right side in the usual position. A small decorated food vessel was found behind the head. The only other objects found in the cist were a splinter of flint, and the burnt tooth of an animal. There were indications, in the curvature of the leg bones, that the child had suffered from rickets.

A pick, made of stag's antler, was found amongst limestone rubble near the primary grave and the end of a similar pick was found in the grave, having doubtless been broken off while excavating the limestone.

It will be seen that the burial places of ancient Britons afford us information as to the appearance and customs of those who were deposited in them. The association of ornaments such as bonepins and brooches may be fairly considered to presuppose the presence of garments, in fact remains of woollen and leather garments have been found in some pre-historic graves. The custom of burying various articles such as weapons, tools, ornaments, and pottery containing food, with the body of the departed may have been done under the impression that the gifts would be useful to the spirit of the dead in another world.

It is interesting to compare the long period of time, since the burials took place on Hasting Hill, with a few outstanding features in history :—
I. In Biographical History, the burial probably took place about the time of Abraham, 2,000 B.C.
2,800 years before the time of Bede (born in Sunderland) 673 A.D.
2,000 years before Cæsar.
1,100 years before David and Solomon.
800 years before Moses.
II. In the History of Nations :—
3,000 years before the landing of William the Conqueror.
Before the Roman Empire, the zenith of Greece, and early in the History of Babylonia.

There is a fine collection of Local pre-historic remains in the model room of the Sunderland Museum.

(1) Under the south window, in a glass case, are the two cists already described, which are set up precisely as found on Hasting Hill.

(2) In the glass wall-case, on the right of the pre-historic remains, are the two British vases found on Humbledon Hill in 1873.

(3) An ancient British dug-out canoe, found in the bed of the river near Hylton in 1885, is placed at the top of the glass cases near the cists. It has been hewn out of an oak tree trunk and is estimated to be more than 2,000 years old.

(4) In the long sloping desk case, near the canoe, are a fine assortment of stone and metal implements used by the ancient Britons.* The gradual development from rough flint weapons to finely polished weapons and tools may be easily traced. The stones used for polishing and shaping the instruments are also exhibited in this case, and it is interesting to notice that the implements are arranged in chronological order; those marked as belonging to the Neolithic and Bronze Ages are such as might have been used in constructing and hollowing the pre-historic canoe.

(5) In the adjoining Museum Gallery is another large case in which are arranged other items from the Hasting Hill barrow, and also pre-historic objects found in the neighbourhood at West Boldon, Ryhope and Fulwell.

* There are 27 books in the Sunderland Public Libraries dealing with Pre-historic man. Some of them contain beautiful illustrations of ancient pottery, stone and bronze implements and other objects.

It is pleasing to find that teachers from different parts of the County, accompanied by their pupils, frequently visit the Museum to examine the admirably arranged collection of British relics.

Pre-Historic Objects from the County of Durham in the British Museum, London.

PLACE.	OBJECTS FOUND.
Barmton, Houghton-le-Skerne (between Barmton and Great Burton)	Late Celtic iron sword with bronze guard and scabbard.
Barnard Castle.	Two gold ornaments.
Copt Hill, Houghton-le-Spring.	Flint scrapers, flakes, bones, etc.
Heathery Burn Cave, Stanhope.	Two bronze cylindrical armlets & disc. Bronze spearhead.
Holwick, Teesdale.	Jet beads.
Sadberge.	Late Celtic iron sword with bronze guard and scabbard.
South Shields.	Two flint knives.
Trimdon Grange.	Cinerary Urn.
Fawnless, Wolsingham.	Bronze palstave.
Hurbeck.	Mould for flat celts.
Sacriston.	Drinking cup with skeleton in cist.
Stone Bridge.	Two Cinerary Urns, food vessel and incense cup. Flat copper celt, bronze palstave.

It is, of course, far beyond the limit of this local history to give anything like a detailed account of Pre-historic times. The first chapter, however, provides many subjects for reflection, and shows that we must not consider the ancient Britons as merely savages, staining their bodies in order, as is said in some history readers, to strike terror into their enemies. Probably the staining of various designs and figures of wild animals on the arms and breasts of the warriors was for the purpose of showing the race or clan to which they belonged, much in the same way, as ages afterwards, an English Knight had his armorial bearings painted on his shield and banner, and as our soldiers of the present day have distinguishing letters and badges on their uniforms to show the regiment to which they belong.

The ancient Britons had coins of their own, which are known to be rude copies of ancient Greek coins; they had acquired many domestic arts, could make baskets, pottery, cloth, and articles from wood, stone and metals; they were skilled fishermen, and could cultivate the land; they had some idea of a future life after death, and having attained to a considerable degree of civilisation were far in advance of a state of barbarism when the Romans first visited our land.

CHAPTER II.

Roman Period.
B.C. 55 to A.D. 410

ANY standard English History will give a general account of the Conquest of Britain by the Romans and of the three hundred and sixty years during which those wonderful people lived in our land. But we have now to consider the Roman Invasion in connection with our own district at the time when the land north of the Humber was occupied by the Brigantes, the most powerful nation of the ancient Britons. According to the Roman historian, Tacitus, they were ruled by a king named Venutus, and the chief city of their kingdom was called Isurium Brigantium. The Brigantes fought long and fiercely against the Romans, and in one expedition against Severus the Romans lost 70,000 men. But the conquerors of the world ultimately prevailed, and the brave Brigantes being at length reduced to subjection (A.D. 80), this part of our land was formed into a Roman province denominated Maxima Caesariensis. Isurium Brigantium was at first the headquarters of the province as it had been the capital of the Brigantes, but afterwards Eboracum (York) was made the headquarters of the Sixth Legion and the seat of the Roman Emperors. Severus, Constantius and his son Constantine, all died at York. How deeply the Roman Empire made its mark on our county, and the difficulties it experienced in subduing the Celtic inhabitants, may be seen by the large number of military camps which were established between the Tees and Tyne.

Military Roads and Towns in Durham
THE Roman camps or towns were all situated on or near the great military road known as Watling Street. This road enters the county at Piercebridge, and proceeding in a northly direction leaves Durham at Ebchester. The village of Piercebridge occupies the site of the Roman town named MAGIS. In the immediate vicinity many Roman altars and the foundations of Roman buildings have been uncovered from time to time, but the only place in our county that has been systematically excavated is the Roman city of VINOVIA, near Binchester. During the excavations which took place in 1877 it was ascertained that VINOVIA had been an important and strongly fortified town in Roman times. Remains of large public buildings were uncovered and a Roman

public bath was found in a fair state of preservation. Paved streets with fountains, altars, and other inscribed stones were numerous, and a Roman pottery with many specimens of earthenware, clay, and colouring substances were brought to light.

The village of Lanchester stands about half a mile from the Roman camp known as LONGOVICUS. The church and many of the houses in the village have been built with stones from the Roman town. Many fine altars were found, seventeen of which were deposited in the Dean and Chapter Library at Durham, and one of great interest, dedicated to the British Goddess Garmangabis, was placed in the church porch at Lanchester. Ebchester occupies the site on which stood the Roman town of VINDOMORA. This old Roman town has provided most of the stones used in the erection of the church and dwellings at Ebchester. There is some uncertainty about the name of the fifth Roman town, situated at Chester-le-Street. It was either called CUNEACESTRE or EPEIAKON by the Romans. A few notable remains of Roman times may be seen in the Church Institute at Chester-le-Street. These include an interesting altar, much defaced, on which are inscribed the words Deabus and Vedra, the former being the name of a local deity of the Celtic period, and the latter the name the Roman historian Ptolemy gives to the Wear.

Another important Roman camp, known as GLANOVENTA, stood near South Shields, and many objects of special interest from this camp are exhibited in the South Shields Library. Roman inscribed stones and coins have also been found at Jarrow and Seaton Carew where Roman stations once stood. Mention has already been made of Watling Street, about eight miles to the east of which was a second Roman road entering Durham at Middleton-one-Row and stretching onwards to the Roman Station of PONS AELII at Newcastle. A third Roman road existed between Lanchester and Chester-le-Street, whence it was continued by an ancient road known as Wreken Dyke to South Shields. There was also a Roman coast road from the Tees to the Tyne, crossing the Wear at Hylton, the only available ford at that period.

Roman Remains in Sunderland and District
There can be no doubt that a Roman station once stood near the mouth of the Wear. Various places have been assigned as the supposed site, but the high ground overlooking the river at the north end of Castle Street has for generations been accepted by local antiquarians and students of history as the most likely place. An ancient building once stood at the place indicated, and in 1873 the late Mr John Moore examined the foundations, which were four feet thick, and found the worked stones and cement were in keeping with Roman workmanship. The ancient well in the district was for centuries known as the Castle Well, and ancient sculptured stones of supposed Roman work have been dug up near it. The ancient building would command a view of the mouth of the river, and not only dominated the passage of the river, thus protecting the fords at Deptford and Hylton, but also possessed great facilities for defence, having the high cliff and the river on the north; the steep sides of the Gill on the west; a deep fissure in the limestone cliff on the east, thus leaving only the south to be protected by a wall and ditch. Recent discoveries tend to strengthen the opinion respecting this

as to the Roman site. About thirty years ago when the River Wear Commissioners' workmen were removing rocks and other impediments to the navigation of the river at Hylton they took from the bed of the river a number of worked stones, amongst which was the keystone of the arch of a bridge supposed to have been erected at the spot by the Romans. The stones were united by iron straps, and both Dr. Bruce, the great authority on Roman antiquities, and the Rev. C. S. Collingwood were of opinion that the stones were of Roman workmanship. An inscribed Roman stone still exists near the place, and the well known antiquary Mr. John Robinson gave particulars about it in an interesting paper on the Ancient Rectory Buildings of Bishopwearmouth, read at a meeting of the Newcastle Society of Antiquaries on the 28th October, 1903. There is not space to give the paper here, but it may be mentioned that the stone may still be seen built into, and forming part of, the wall of the coach-house which belonged to the ancient Rectory. The stone is five feet seven inches long and twelve inches wide, and the Roman capitals V S L M are cut into it. The letters stand for the Roman words Votum, Solvit, Libens, Merito, and mean " In discharge of a vow willingly and deservedly made." It seems evident that the stone once formed the base of a Roman altar, and that it and other suitable stones were collected from the site of the Roman station and used in the erection of the old Rectory.

Roman coins have been found at Sunderland, Fulwell and Whitburn, and a number of ancient Roman chisels were discovered in the crevices of the stone in a quarry near Bishopwearmouth. In 1759 two Roman coins, a cinerary urn, and a gigantic human skeleton, nine feet six inches in length, were found in an ancient barrow on the Fulwell Hills. From the description given in Summers' History it is evident that there had been two burials in this barrow, the first during the Bronze age and the other during the Roman period. The coins were found near the right hand of the skeleton. In Roman graves coins were usually placed in the mouth or right hand of the deceased, and are referred to as "Charon's passage fee." It was thought that the coins would expedite the passage of the soul across the river in Hades, and that the person who had not received the usual rites of burial, and had no fee for Charon, the ferryman of the Styx, would wander hopelessly on the banks of the river. Another Roman grave, uncovered in 1820 whilst working the Carley Hill Quarry, Fulwell, was found to contain, in addition to human remains, a Roman domestic or household god, called a Lare. It was presented by Dr. Clanny to the Newcastle Society of Antiquaries. Particulars of a Roman pottery discovered at Sunderland are given in Chapter XII.

Roman Altars found in Weardale WEARDALE appears to have been well known to the Romans, who enjoyed hunting in the great Weardale forest. In 1747 a Roman altar was found on Bollihope Fell, near Stanhope. It bears an interesting inscription relating to a sporting feat of a Roman officer. The translation of the Latin inscription is as follows :—

"Sacred to the Unconquered Silvanus. Caius Veturius Micianus, prefect of the Sebosian wing, on account of a boar of enormous size, which was captured, which many of his predecessors were unable to take, gladly placed (this altar) discharging his vow." The altar is now in the Rectory at Stanhope.

In 1869 another Roman altar was discovered near Eastgate. This also was dedicated to Silvanus, the god of the woods, by Aurelius Quirinus, Prefect of Rome, who was stationed with his cohort of the Gordian Legion at Lanchester, A.D. 236-244. Other Roman antiquities found in Weardale include Roman querns, brass spearheads, Roman silver coins, and remains of Roman lead ore smelting works.

Roman Remains in Black Gate Museum Newcastle   THE finest collection of Roman antiquities of this neighbourhood is to be seen in the Black Gate Museum at Newcastle. The building was erected as part of the Norman Castle, by Henry III., in 1247. It is now used by the Newcastle Society of Antiquities as a Museum and may be justly described as a treasure house of pre-historic and Roman remains.

The first room contains Roman objects from the district of the Roman Wall and from several Roman camps in the County of Durham. There are more than two hundred Roman inscribed stones on view, including altars dedicated to Mithras, the sun god; Neptune, Mercury, Jupiter, Fortune, Silvanus, Mars, and Victory. Some of them are inscribed with the names of Roman Emperors and particulars of Roman Legions. There are several sepulchral tablets of great interest. One was erected by a Roman soldier "To his devoted mother"; another stone bears the inscription "To his dearest daughter." These memorial stones have the letters S T T L at the foot, and these letters stand for the Roman words *Sit Tibi Terra Levis, i.e.*, "May earth rest light on thee."

There are three glass cases in this room containing Roman iron arrow heads and other implements;

examples of the stylus, an instrument with a sharp point used for writing on tablets covered with wax; gold necklace, finger rings, Roman pottery, coins, and other articles of use or ornament.

The second room contains thirty-three large glass cases containing complete collections of Cinerary urns and other pre-historic pottery; bronze weapons and tools; stone implements; Roman lamps and bronze vessels; gold, jet and bronze jewellery of fine workmansnip. Six of the glass cases are devoted to the Blair collection of Roman objects from the Roman station at South Shields.

This splendid collection, which represents the work of many years, is of great educational value, and must be seen to be appreciated. No written account can possibly do justice to the light it throws on Roman times in this district.

Ancient Britons under the Roman Rule AFTER the conquest of the Britons, and when the different tribes were reduced to a state of submission, the Romans turned their attention to the improvement of the agriculture and commerce of our island. They drained marshes, built bridges, and intersected the country with well made Roman roads. They introduced many beautiful flowers as well as the lime, chestnut, walnut, cherry, and apple trees, and taught the methods of grafting fruit trees. The natives were encouraged to devote themselves to profitable industries; immense quantities of corn were grown and exported, and our island received the name of "The Granary of the North." In the year A.D. 359, five vessels sailed from Britain with corn to succour the Roman colonies on the Rhine, which had been plundered by the Huns. Merchants from France, Italy, and Greece were encouraged to visit and trade with Britain. The imports were of a most varied character and included ivory, gold ornaments, beautiful ware and glass, fine clothing, leather goods, etc. The exports consisted of tin, copper, lead, pearls, jet, corn, sheep, furs, skins, and slaves.

The island was well protected against foreign aggression; in the north, from the Tyne to the Solway, was the wonderful Roman Wall with its mile-castles and garrisons, and round the coast were maritime stations and ships to prevent invasions of the Saxons who made several attempts to gain a landing.

Thus the Britons gradually came under Roman law and the richer and more ambitious natives were drawn to the towns where they learned to live, speak, and dress like the Romans, and at last became proud of being Roman subjects; but in the country districts they never gave up their Celtic language or their national mode of life. We must not forget that Christianity was first introduced into our land during the Roman occupation. We learn from Irenaeus, who was Bishop of Lyons about the year A.D. 178, that the light of the gospel had at that time dawned in Britain. The first British martyr for the faith was Alban, who was put to death on the 20th of June, 304. Christianity, however, was not encouraged by the State till the year 324, when the Emperor Constantine, himself a Christian, exhorted his subjects to follow his example and abandon the errors of paganism. Constantine was the first Roman Emperor to become a Christian. He is said to have been born in Britain, and his mother Helen to have been a Briton.[*]

We can dimly picture the vast changes which the Roman occupation must have wrought in our district.

[*] Old English History, by E. A. Freeman, D.C.L.

MONKWEARMOUTH CHURCH PRIOR TO 1874.

Pathless forests and dreary swamps had in a great measure been replaced by fertile well-ordered farms; the rude huts of the Britons had given way to stately well-built towns with busy markets and no inconsiderable manufactures; the people, at any rate in the towns, had advanced to a higher degree of civilisation; and, best of all, the blessings of Christianity had dispelled the cruelties and errors of the dark days of heathenism. It is sad to reflect that all this material and moral progress was so soon to be swept away by the hands of fierce and cruel invaders.

CHAPTER III.

SUNDERLAND IN SAXON AND DANISH TIMES.
449 TO 1066.

The Saxon Kingdom of Northumbria
From the time the Romans left England until the establishment of the Saxon kingdom of Northumbria, by Ida in 547, the history of our district is little more than a continuous record of the incursions of the Scots and Picts and of the struggle with the Anglo-Saxons.

Ida subdued the inhabitants of the northern parts of England and established the kingdom of Bernicia while Ella, another Saxon prince, overcame Durham and part of Yorkshire, and received the appellation of King of Deira. These two kingdoms were afterwards united and named Northumbria (one of the Heptarchy, or seven Saxon kingdoms). From the year 547 to 800 Northumbria was ruled over by about thirty kings. One of these, King Oswald, introduced Christianity into our district through the influence of the monk Aidan, who founded the See of Lindisfarne.

Cuthbert, often spoken of as the great saint of Northumbria, became the sixth Bishop of Lindisfarne. He was so highly distinguished for his purity of life and manners that immense gifts were conferred upon the church for his sake. Cuthbert died on the 20th March, 687, and when his body was removed from Lindisfarne to Chester-le-Street, Guthred, king of Northumbria, made a gift of all the land between the Wear and the Tyne for a perpetual possession. Such was the commencement of the privileges and immunities which eventually converted the patrimony of St. Cuthbert into the County Palatine of Durham and exalted its Bishops to the high estate of temporal princes.

Northumbria ceased to exist as a separate and independent kingdom when Egbert became king of England in the year 800.

The Abbot Biscop and the Priest Bede THE history of Sunderland during the Saxon times is closely connected with the lives of Biscop and Bede. Benedict Biscop was descended from a noble Anglican family. For several years he was in the service of King Oswin. When twenty-five years of age he decided to devote his life to the service of God, and after visiting Rome to study monastic life, he entered a monastery near Cannes, in France, where he remained for two years. After a second visit to Rome he returned to England, and for two years had charge of St. Peter's monastery at Canterbury. He once more went to Rome in order to purchase sacred books and relics, after which he returned to Northumbria, where Egfrid, the son of Oswin, had become king, and there he zealously set about instructing his countrymen in the learning and religious discipline in which he had himself been trained.

Monastic Houses erected at Monkwearmouth & Jarrow IN the year 674, Egfrid gave Biscop seventy hides of land (about 7,000 acres) at the mouth of the Wear, on the left bank, and ordered a monastery to be built thereon. Biscop at once commenced the erection of monastic buildings, and a church which was dedicated to St. Peter. The structure was built of stone in what was called the Roman style, then prevalent throughout Western Europe, being an adaptation of the old classical Roman *forum*. Biscop visited France himself in order to engage skilled masons and such was the diligence of the workmen that they had nearly finished the work in the course of a year. Makers of glass were also brought from the Continent in order that they might glaze the windows not only of the church and its aisles and chancels, but of the cloisters and dining room of the monastery. Monkwearmouth has thus the honour of being the first place in England where glass was made. In the year 678 Benedict Biscop set out on a journey to Rome in order to purchase books, vessels, vestments, images and pictures for the church. He also obtained the services of John the Arch-chanter and Abbot of St. Martin at Rome, who returned with him to instruct the monks in music and ritual according to Roman use.

In the year 681 King Egfrid granted an additional forty hides of land, on the south side of the Tyne, to the Abbot Benedict, for the erection of a sister monastic house. Benedict at once commenced the work of building a monastery and church at Jarrow, and in the following year Ceolfrid, as Abbot, and seventeen monks were transferred from St. Peter's to Jarrow. In 683

Biscop made his fifth and last visit to Rome for more treasures for his monasteries.

He returned after an absence of four years with a large collection of books, pictures, relics, and other valuable ecclesiastical treasures. During his absence the church at Jarrow had been completed and dedicated to St. Paul, on the 24th April, 684; King Egfrid had been slain in battle in 685, and a large number of monks had died of pestilence.

An event of special local interest is connected with Biscop's last journey to Rome, as among the articles he brought back were two beautiful cloaks woven entirely of silk, and in exchange for these he obtained from King Alfred three hides of land near the mouth, on the south bank, of the Wear.

The land thus obtained was called by the monks "Sondralande," which means separated-land, because it was separated from the larger estate of the monastery which stood on the north bank of the river and stretched from the Wear to the Tyne.

The name, however, may also be accounted for by the fact that the land was almost separated, or sundered, from the mainland by the Wear and the sea, hence again we have the Saxon name "Sondralande," or, as we call it, Sunderland.

The Abbot Benedict Biscop died at the monastery at Monkwearmouth on the 12th of January, 690. He was the founder and first abbot and had ruled the monastery for 16 years. His remains were interred in the church of St. Peter's until the year 694, when the Bishop of Winchester purchased the bones of Biscop for a great sum of money and conveyed them to his new Abbey at Thorney, in Cambridgeshire.

Bede was born at Sunderland in 672, and when seven years of age was admitted to the monastery at Monkwearmouth. In 683 he accompanied Ceolfrid and the monks to Jarrow.

When 19 years of age he was ordained Deacon, and 11 years afterwards he became a Priest.

He spent the whole of his life in the monastery and became the most remarkable scholar of his time. He diligently applied himself to the service of the church and his chief delight was in learning, in teaching, and in writing. He instructed nearly six hundred students who had been drawn to Jarrow by his fame as a teacher. He wrote fifty books, mostly concerned with religion. The works of local interest were:—"A Life of Bishop Cuthbert," and "The History of the Three Abbots of Jarrow—Benedict, Ceolfrid, and Huetbert."

The most important of his works was "The Ecclesiastical History of England." King Alfred the Great thought so highly of this book that he translated it out of the Latin, in which it was written by Bede, into the English tongue. Bede has justly been called "The father of English learning" as he was the first Englishman of letters, the first church historian, and the first man of science.

To him we are indebted for almost all our information on the ancient history of England down to the year 731 A.D.

It is most interesting to record that 1203 years ago, on the 4th of June, 716, Ceolfrid, the Abbot of the united monasteries of Monkwearmouth and Jarrow, left Sunderland with a few companions in order to visit the city of Rome. He took with him as a present to Pope Gregory II. one of the three "Pandects," or whole Bibles, which he had caused to be made (probably under the direction of Bede) at Jarrow, from the Vulgate translation of the Bible.

Ceolfrid died on his journey, at Langres, in France. His fellow monks, however, proceeded to Rome, and laid the gift of Ceolfrid, with its dedication verses, at the foot of the Holy Father.

Nothing more was heard of the Northumbrian manuscript until about thirty years ago, when De Rossi, the famous historian of the Catacombs of Rome, made the discovery that the magnificent copy of the Vulgate Bible, the celebrated "Codex Amiatinus" in the Laurentian Library in Florence, was actually the Northumbrian manuscript.

This is the most valuable manuscript now existing of the ancient Latin version of the Bible. It has been described as "Perhaps the finest book in the world," and is famous for its beautiful writing and gorgeous illuminations.

Bede died on the 27th of May, 735, and his remains were interred in St. Paul's Church, Jarrow. In 1020 his bones were removed to Durham Cathedral, and are now deposited in the beautiful Galilee or Lady Chapel. A plain stone covers the spot and bears the inscription:—

HERE REST THE BONES OF VENERABLE BEDE.

For the sake of continuity further particulars of Bede and our ancient churches are included here.

The buildings erected by Biscop at Jarrow and Monkwearmouth were almost totally destroyed by the Danes in 867, and nothing more is known respecting Monkwearmouth monastery until the year 1074, when Walcher, the Norman Bishop of Durham, gave the ruined monastery and church to Aldwine, a former Prior of Winchelcomb, in Worcestershire.

The monks found the walls of the church overgrown with brambles and thorns, but they were cleared away and the building repaired and covered with a roof, and divine services were in a short time restored to it. Thus it continued till 1083, when the Bishop of Durham removed the Benedictine monks from Monkwearmouth and Jarrow to Durham.

From that time the monastery of Monkwearmouth became a dependent cell of the great convent of Durham until the suppression of the lesser religious houses in 1538. Although these ancient churches have frequently been restored and added to, they still contain parts of the original structures.*

At St. Peter's, the west of the nave, the western porch, and the lower part of the tower are all parts of the original church. The eight curious lathe-turned balusters, which remain in the same position as they were placed by Biscop's masons in 674, are a remarkable feature of the building. In the vestry, a modern erection, are preserved numerous fragments of finely carved stones belonging to the ancient church. There is also a Saxon tombstone bearing the inscription :—

  HERE IN THE SEPULCHRE RESTS IN THE BODY
    THE PRIEST HERBERT.

The beautiful stained glass windows in St. Peter's Church are very interesting, being connected with local Saxon history. The figures represent St. Aidan, St. Benedict, St. Paulinus, The Venerable Bede, St. Cuth-

* "The Church of St. Peter's," by J. Patterson, gives a full account.

bert, St. Oswald, St. Hilda, and St. Edwin, and below each figure is a representation of the most important event in the life of each saint. Nothing remains of the ancient monastery of Monkwearmouth, on the site of which a large mansion was built in the time of King James I. Monkwearmouth Hall, as it was called, was completely destroyed by fire on the 13th April, 1790, and with it perished those portions of the hall which had once formed part of the monastic building.

The stained glass windows in St. Paul's Church, Jarrow, represent the death of Bede, and there are other objects connected with his life to be seen at Jarrow.

The Bede Memorial Cross THE people of Sunderland have erected the Bede Cross, at Roker, in honour of one of their famous sons. On one side are extracts from Bede's works, and beneath the four sculptured lines runs, in a band, the verse written by Bede on his death-bed.

When this beautiful cross was unveiled, in 1904, by Dr. Maclagan, Archbishop of York, he said :—" It has been erected to a great memory, the memory of a great scholar, a great historian, a great theologian, a great lover and interpreter of the word of God, of one who was in the highest sense a man of letters, but, above all, a man of God."

When we look at the beautiful Anglican Cross erected to the memory of the Venerable Bede we are reminded that the Cross originally pointed out the spots where Christianity was first preached to our forefathers, and near which the churches were usually erected. It afterwards became part of the decorations of every church, in order to inspire reverence. In former days there were numerous wayside crosses in England. On commons and moors, which often stretched for miles without a fence on either side, it was necessary to set up marks of some kind for travellers. Our forefathers chose the symbol of Christian religion for their guide, and set it up here and there by the wayside for the purpose of calling the thoughts of travellers to a sense of religion and for restraining the predatory incursions of robbers. In the market place the Cross was a symbol for upright intention and fair dealing, and in every place it was designed as a check to a worldly spirit and to intimate that all the transactions of life were to be under the controlling influence of the doctrine and example of Christ. At the reformation many crosses were ruthlessly destroyed, and about the year 1640, at the time of the Great Rebellion, the remainder disappeared almost everywhere.

The Sunderland market cross disappeared from High Street, where the markets were held, about this time. There are still many wayside crosses in France, and in our own country many may be restored on village greens and other places in memory of our brave soldiers who gave their lives for Freedom and Justice during the Great War of 1914 to 1918. Maps published by Speed in 1610 marked the spots where churchyard, market, and wayside crosses were erected in our county.

Danish Incursions and Settlement AFTER the death of Bede, in 735, a dense cloud of darkness overshadows the history of Sunderland. The Danish incursions on the Northumbrian coast began towards the end of the eighth century and continued, at intervals, for over 200 years. In 793, the monastery and church at Lindisfarne were plundered and burnt, and in the following year the religious buildings at Jarrow

D

suffered a similar fate. On this occasion, however, the English inhabitants of the Tyne and Wear united their forces and drove the invaders to their ships, after killing one of the Danish leaders. Some of the ships were then wrecked by a tempest, and many of the Danes were drowned or driven ashore and slain at the mouth of the Tyne.

This repulse at Jarrow had the effect or checking these descents on our coast for nearly 100 years, and then the war vessels of the Danish sea rover, Ragner Lodbrog, appeared off the mouth of the Wear. His fleet was shattered by a storm, and many of the vessels were driven ashore near Hendon.

A great conflict took place between the English and Danes at Elleshope,* a valley near Tunstall Hills, when the latter were defeated and their leader captured and put to death.

In 867, Inguar and Hubba, the sons of Ragner Lodbrog, came, with an immense number of followers, to avenge the death of their father and to plunder the whole of Northumbria. The barbarians overcame all opposition and committed the most cruel excesses; they set fire to the houses and churches, after plundering them of everything of value, and put the miserable inhabitants to the sword without distinction of age or sex.

An old English Chronicler, Roger de Wendover, states that the noblest of the monasteries along the Northumbrian coast were destroyed by these pirates and he especially mentions Lindisfarne, Tynemouth, Jarrow, Wearmouth, and Whitby as having suffered at their hands.

*This valley lies between Tunstall Road and Silksworth Road, and in it are Elstob farm and the Hope Gardens.

The heavy calamities under which our district suffered met with no redress until the reign of Alfred. How the Danish power was driven back by this great Saxon king, and how by his wise policy he reclaimed half of his kingdom is a well known part of our national history.

A hundred and sixteen years after the death of Alfred, England was completely subject to the dominion of the Danes, and from 1016 to 1042 Danish kings held sway in England.

Canute, the best of the Danish kings, strove successfully to blend the two races over whom he ruled, and gradually the Danes became a changed people. They settled down on the land, inter-married with the Angles and Saxons, and the two races eventually became one people. It is thus that the Danish invaders became settlers. In our district the English people retained the land which they never ceased to occupy. There are few Danish names to be found in Sunderland district. The names Suddick (Southwick) and Biddick possibly suggest that bands of Danes originally settled in these places and gave to them the names they still retain.

According to local tradition Galley Gill marks the place where Danish invaders found shelter for their vessels when plundering our district in remote ages. When the Lambton Coal staiths were made, the remains of a Danish galley were discovered embedded in the ground at the base of the limestone cliff in the old Gill.

The harbour at the mouth of the river Wear, "Wiranmuthan," or "Sundorlande" as Bede calls it, was well known in Saxon and Danish times. It was undoubtedly much frequented, both on account of the maritime conveniences it afforded to the small vessels which then navigated the coast, and on account of the celebrated monastery which stood on the northern bank of the river.

Athel=stan's gift to the See of Durham. THE first mention of South Wearmouth, or which we have any record, appears about the year 930 when King Athelstan visited the shrine of St. Cuthbert, at Chester-le-Street, and gave or restored South Wearmouth to the See of Durham. The grant included Westoe, Offerton, Silksworth, the two Ryhopes, Burdon, Seaham, Seaton, Dalton, Dalden, and Haseldene. King Athelstan spoke of the town as "My pleasant vill of South Wearmouth."

After this gift the little town became known as Bishop-Wearmouth, to show that it formed part of the Bishop's possessions and to distinguish it from Monk Wearmouth which belonged to the Monks of the Benedictine Monastery.

About the year 940 a church, dedicated to St. Michael, was built at Bishopwearmouth. Some of the ancient stones from this early Saxon building are to be seen in the present church (erected in 1807), and on one of these stones are the deep, narrow, cuttings made by the ancient archers when sharpening their arrow heads.

Bishopwearmouth Church has had a long succession of learned Rectors who faithfully administered to the spiritual needs of the town. Many of them attained very high positions in our National Church. The list includes three Cardinals, three Archbishops, seven Bishops, and the famous Archdeacon Paley, D.D., the author of "Evidences of Christianity."

A few Saxon coins have been found in this district. Twelve "Stycas," belonging to the time of Ecgfrith

(670-685), were discovered at Gateshead in 1822, and four silver pennies of Alfred's reign were found at Gainford in 1865.

In 1815 a curious brooch or buckle, of the Saxon period, was discovered in an ancient grave at East Boldon. It is ornamented with three small circular bosses of gold which enclose three polished garnets. This brooch was presented by the late Rev. G. C. Abbs, of Cleadon, to the Newcastle Museum of Antiquaries.

The most beautiful of the Anglo-Saxon relics found in our county was a bluish-green glass bowl found in a Saxon burial-place at Castle Eden in 1775.

During the reign of Harold, the last of the Saxon kings, on the site which the town of Sunderland now occupies stood the three little villages or hamlets of Wearmouth, Bishop Wearmouth, and Monkwearmouth, and we shall endeavour to trace, through the intervening centuries, their growth and progress, culminating in our present prosperous town of Sunderland.

Bishop-wearmouth in Saxon Times   LET us try to picture Bishopwearmouth as it appeared a thousand years ago. On the crest of the hill stands the small Saxon church, made of wood, the roof thatched with reeds.

On three sides of the church are clustered the dwelling houses, each with a small croft, and garden with fruit trees; while on the fourth side is the village green where men and boys practised at the butts.

Surrounding the town may be seen a ditch and an earthen wall, with a wooden fence on top, as a defence against any enemy.

Very early in the morning the town gate is opened and the herd appears driving the villagers' cattle, which he has collected from each croft, to the grass land at Boyldon Hill.

Next appear the Ceorls, the most numerous and the lowest class of Saxon freemen. They are accompanied by a number of Thralls or slaves, and are on their way to the strips of cultivated land at the west of the village where wheat, rye, oats, and barley are grown. Now we see the Thane with his sons and house carls issue forth. Some follow the stream which joins the Wear and are going to fish for salmon; others are going to hunt in the woods.

An extensive view of the sea and the surrounding country can be obtained from the village as none of the land is enclosed. There are no noisy shipyards, no busy factories belching forth smoke from their tall chimneys, and the Wear runs swiftly to the sea between steep, craggy banks, in parts overgrown with bushes and trees. In place of the tiers of great tramp steamers, a few long black galleys ride at anchor and here and there a rude boat is drawn up on the shore.

CHAPTER IV.

SUNDERLAND IN NORMAN AND PLANTAGENET TIMES.
1066 TO 1485.

The Normans Invade Durham Two years elapsed, after the Battle of Hastings, before the Normans obtained any footing in the County of Durham. Before this took place, however, Edgar Atheling, the heir to the English throne, with his sister and a number of Saxon followers, took refuge in the port of Sunderland, waiting for a favourable wind to carry them to Scotland.

Bishopwearmouth in 1810.

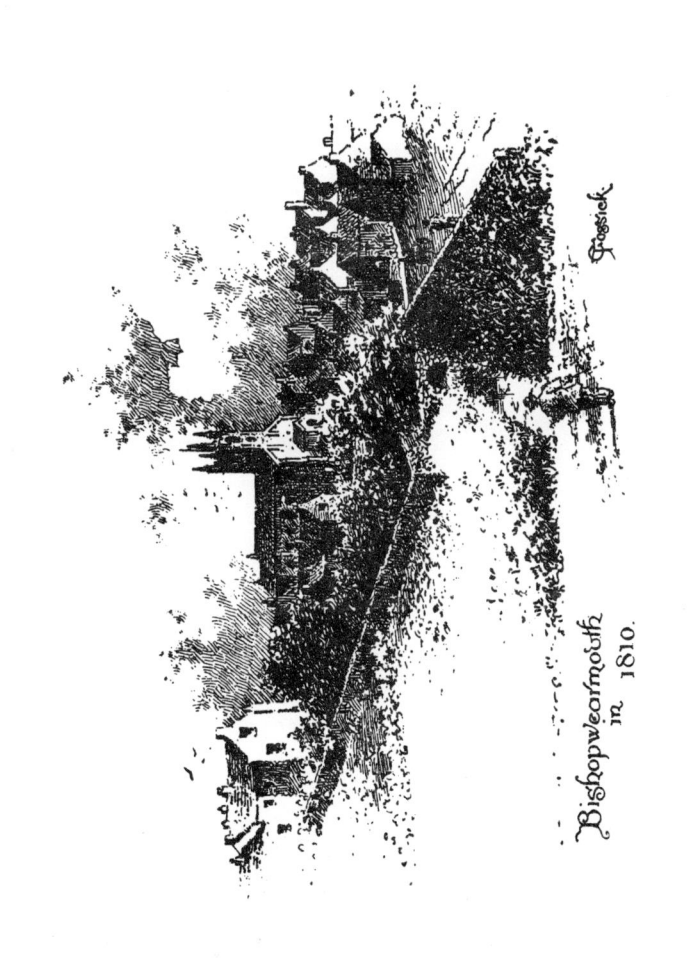

It is recorded that Malcolm III., King of Scotland, overran the whole of Northumbria, bore away from the mouth of the Wear Edgar Atheling and Margaret, his sister, whom he made his wife—the Saint Margaret of Scotland—and burnt a church on the banks of the Wear. In the following year, 1069, William I. appointed Robert Comyn as Earl of Northumberland, but when he entered the city of Durham, with his body guard of nine hundred Norman soldiers, he was opposed by the English, who declined to submit to the Norman rule, and after a severe battle the whole of the Normans, including Comyn, were slain.

A larger force of Norman soldiers soon entered the county and so completely routed the insurgents and devastated the district that it is said that not a house south of Durham city was left standing; even churches and monasteries were burnt, and the land was laid waste from the Tees to the Tyne.

Three years after this disaster the last of the Saxon bishops of Durham died and he was succeeded by Walcher, a native of Lorraine. He also became Earl of Northumberland, and may be regarded as the first of the great Prince Bishops of Durham who had all the rights and privileges of a King within the county.

Bishop Walcher governed Durham and Northumberland for eight years, but unfortunately two of his Norman officials put to death a Saxon nobleman called Lyulph, the ancestor of the old Durham family of Lumley. This was the immediate cause of a second rising against the Normans, and the Bishop with a number of his followers was slain at Gateshead.

We must remember that the Normans in England were a dominant minority and had to guard against the insurrections of a subjugated people, and therefore this second rising led to another devastation by Norman soldiers and the whole county was left so impoverished and depopulated that its non-appearance in Domesday Book (compiled in 1085) is supposed to be due to this cause. The people then living at Sunderland would suffer equally with the inhabitants of Gateshead and other parts of Durham.

How the land was held in Norman Times A change now took place in the settlement of the land throughout the county, on a feudal basis, and the Bishop of Durham parcelled out his land into manors and these were granted to adherents of the Conqueror. The holder of a manor in turn parcelled out his holding. The best site was naturally chosen for the residence of the Lord of the Manor and the adjoining land, called the Demesne, was retained for his own cultivation.

Next came holdings of various sizes which were let oft to the lord's followers, and the condition of their service was either an annual money payment or military service in time of war. These tenants constituted the freeholders of the Manor. Next came the Villeins who occupied land purely at the will of the lord of the Manor and instead of paying rent they had to perform services of a personal nature, such as cultivating the land of the Demesne, attending the lord when hunting, or providing eggs and fowls for their lord.

The Villeins cultivated their own plots of land when their services were not required by their lord.

The rest of the land of the Manor was called *waste* and was used as a common pasture for horses and cattle. The lord provided the mill and it was usual for him to provide a stock of cattle and the necessary implements of agriculture for the use of his tenants. The smith and carpenter were also provided by the lord, and paid either in land or by a contribution levied on the tenants who were obliged to employ them. All were compelled to grind their corn at the manor mill. The common pasture of Bishopwearmouth consisted of the village green, the land near the burn (afterwards called the Burn Fields), and the pasturage on the Boyldon Hill.

At Sunderland the common pasture, about eighty acres, was called the Town Moor.

The Hilton Family THE most important family living in this district during Norman and Plantagenet times was that of the Hiltons. The Manor of Hilton, in the reign of King Athelstan, was in the possession of Sir William Hilton whose son, Adam Hilton, gave to the monastery of Hartlepool, in the year 924, a silver crucifix which weighed twenty-five ounces.

An old writer relates that upon the coming over of William the Norman, in 1066, Lancelot de Hilton with his two sons, Henry and Robert, espoused his cause and joined him; but that Lancelot was slain at Faversham, in Kent; that to the elder son, Henry, the Conqueror gave a large tract of land on the banks of the river Wear, not far from Wearmouth, as a reward for his own and his father's valour, and that Henry built a castle on the land in the year 1072.

The names of the Barons of Hilton appear from time to time as witnesses of Charters, deeds, agreements and other documents connected with the county of Durham and the town of Sunderland.

The Hiltons also took an active part in national

affairs; Robert Hilton was a member of the first English Parliament and represented the County Palatine during the reign of Edward I.

Another member of the family, Alexander Hilton, attended Parliament in the reign of Edward III.

Sir Thomas Hilton was one of the leaders of the religious rising of 1534 known as the Pilgrimage of Grace, and during the reign of Queen Mary he was governor of Tynemouth Castle.

John Hilton was an officer in the Royal Army during the Civil War, and it was owing to the money he gave to King Charles that the Hilton family became impoverished.

For many generations the Hiltons and their retainers from Wearside maintained themselves in arms and fought bravely for their king and country. One member of the family was slain at Faversham; one in Normandy; one at Metz, in France; three in the Crusade under Richard I., and one in the Crusade under Edward I.; three at the battle of Bordeaux, under the Black Prince; one at Agincourt; two at Berwick against the Scots; two at the battle of St. Albans; five at Market Bosworth and four at Flodden.

From the year 1157 until 1739 there is an unbroken record of this Wearside family, but in the latter year John Hylton, the last male representative of the line, died, and the estates passed to his nephew, Sir Richard Musgrave, of Hayton Castle, who took the name of Hylton and eventually sold the Hylton estates in 1750. These estates were at one time of vast extent and included a total of thirteen manors in Durham, Northumberland, Yorkshire and Cumberland. For more than 600 years Hylton Castle was the home of the Hyltons and nearly all the land that could be seen from the castle belonged to this powerful family. Their descendants no longer dwell in the ancient castle; their possessions are in other hands; and in the locality in which at one time their family were the most powerful and the most honoured they are almost forgotten.

Bishop Pudsey's Charter AN event of great importance to our town was the granting of a Charter of Privileges, by Bishop Pudsey, about the year 1154. The Norman kings endeavoured to create cities and ports in all parts of England, and in order to make new towns popular and to increase trade they granted Charters containing certain privileges to the inhabitants. The Bishops of Durham, following the example set by the Norman kings, granted similar Charters to towns and ports in the county of Durham.

Many who read this book will be interested in reading a translation of the Charter granted by Bishop Hugh Pudsey to the Burgesses of Weremue.

Hugh, by the grace of God, Bishop of Durham.

To the Prior, Archdeacons, Barons, and all the men in the whole of his diocese, both French and English, Greeting. Be it known that we, by this present charter, concede and confirm to our burgesses of Weremue, free customs in their borough, similar to the customs of the burgesses of Newcastle, namely:—

1. That it is lawful for them to judge in a court of law peasants and other rural inhabitants, within their borough if they be indebted to them, without the license of the Bailiff, unless perhaps they may have been placed there by the Bishop or Sheriff, for some matter of the Bishop's own.

2. If a burgess accredited anything to a villein (bondman) within the Borough, and if he deny the debt, it shall be settled within the Borough. However a burgess must not on any reason harass a villein by unlawful speech.

3. All pleas arising within the Borough except those of the Crown, shall be determined there.

4. *If any burgess be accused within the Borough, he must comply, unless he makes his escape into another Borough, when he shall be retained or placed in security, but if the same Borough do not fail in their duty, and if the plea does not pertain to the Crown, he shall not be called upon to answer within an appointed day, unless it has been formerly fixed by an unwise council in law.*

5. *If a ship touch at Weremue, and is about to depart, any Burgesses may purchase whatever merchandise he wishes from the ship, if anyone be willing to sell to him; and if a dispute arise between the burgess and the merchant, they must settle it within the third influx of the tide.*

6. *Merchandise being brought into the Borough by sea, ought to be landed, except salt and herrings, which may be sold either in the ship or in the Borough, at the will of the seller.*

7. *Should anyone hold land in the borough for one year and a day without accusation, while the claimant has been within the realm, and not under age, if then accused he ought not to give it up.*

8. *If a burgess has his son boarded in his own house, the son may enjoy the same liberties as his father.*

9. *If a villein come to live in the Borough and hold land and tenements for a year and a day without accusation, by desire of his landlord, he may remain to any time in the Borough as a burgess.*

10. *It is lawful for a burgess to sell his lands, and go where he pleases, unless his lands be under a bond.*

11. *If a burgess be complained against, in a matter where battle ought to be waged, by a villein or free inhabitant, he may defend or clear himself by the civil law, or by the oath of thirty-six men, unless the value in suit be one hundred pounds, or the crime imputed to him ought to be tried by battle.*

12. *A burgess ought not to fight against a villein if he should force him, unless before the accusation he should have forfeited his office as a burgess.*

13. *Blodwite,* nor Merchet,† nor Heriot,‡ nor Stengesduit,§ ought not to exist in the Borough.*

* A fine paid as a composition for the shedding of blood.

† A payment made by a villein to his lord for liberty to give his daughter in marriage.

‡ A tribute or fine payable to the lord of the fee on the decease of the owner, landowner, or vassal.

§ A fine inflicted for an assault committed with a stick or similar instrument.

14. It is lawful for any burgess to have his own oven and handmill, saving the right of the Lord Bishop.

15. If anyone fall into forfeiture to the Bailiff touching bread or beer, the Bailiff alone can allow him to escape, but if he fall the third time let justice be administered to him by the common consent of the burgesses.

16. A burgess may bring in his corn from the country when he pleases, except at a time of prohibition or embargo.

17. A burgess may give or sell his land to whom he pleases, without the voice or consent of his heir, if he bought it with his own money.

18. Every burgess is at liberty to buy timber and firewood equally with the burgesses of Durham.

19. The burgesses may enjoy their common pasturage, as was originally granted to them, and which we have caused to be perambulated.

20. We shall hold the same customs arising from fish being sold at Weremue as Robert de Brus held from his people at Hartlepool.

21. We will therefore and more firmly determine that the burgesses have and hold the before mentioned customs and privileges freely, quietly, and honourably from us and our successors.

These being Witnesses:—

GERMANUS, *Prior of Durham.*
BURCHARD, *Archdeacon of Durham.*
SYMON, *Treasurer of Durham.*
RICHARD DE COLDINGHAM, *Vicar of St. Oswald's.*
MASTER STEPHEN LINCOLN.
MASTER BERNARD.
HENRY MARESCALL.
ARNOLD ADAM and SIMON, *Chaplains.*
GILBERT DE LEY.
PHILIP THE SHERIFF.
JORDAN ESCOLLAND, *Lord of Dalton.*
ALEXANDER DE HYLTON, *Baron of Hylton.*
GAUFRID, son of RICHARD, *Lord of Horton.*
ROGER DE EPPLETON; and others.

This charter may be considered as the first authentic evidence of the existence of our town as a place of maritime commerce, and it was well calculated to foster the trade of the Borough, by releasing the burgesses from several of the most oppressive parts of the feudal law, by facilitating the transfer of property; providing for the speedy administration of justice; and protecting the feudal slave or stranger who had settled within the Borough, and preventing him from being driven from the town.

Boldon Book, 1180 ABOUT twenty-six years after the Charter had been granted to the Burgesses of Weremue, Bishop Pudsey caused a survey of the possessions of the Palatine to be made, with an account of the tenants by whom the land was held, and the rent or services they rendered. Boldon, a village near Sunderland, is the first place mentioned in the survey and the customs and services of the tenants are set out in full while in other Manors it is simply stated that the services and dues there are similar to those rendered at Boldon, where that is the case, and set out in full where they differ. "Boldon" occurring so frequently, the book containing the particulars of the survey came to be spoken of as the Boldon Book.

In this book are two entries which refer to the area now occupied by our town:—

"In Wearmouth (Bishopwearmouth) and Tunstall are twenty-two tenants in villeinage; and six cottagers, whose work, rents, and services are like those of Boldon. The carpenter, who is aged, holds twelve acres for life, for making carts and harrows for the tenants. The smith has twelve acres and finds his own coal. The pay and services of the Pounder are the same as the Pounder of Boldon, *i.e.*, a landed salary of twelve acres and a thrave of corn from every cart-load, and he pays eighty hens and five hundred eggs annually to the Bishop's Bailiff.

The two vills pay twenty shillings for cornage, or cattle tax, and provide two milch cows. The demesne is farmed with a stock of twenty draught-oxen, two harrows, and two hundred sheep, the rent including the mill is twenty pounds; the fisheries pay six pounds and the Borough of Wearmouth pays twenty shillings; Sunderland is at farm and renders a hundred shillings; Roger, the son of Andres, renders for his mill dam upon the land of Sunderland thirteen shillings and fourpence."

No particulars of Monkwearmouth are given in Boldon Book as the lands there belonged to the Priory of Durham, as successors to the Monastery of Monkwearmouth; nor is any mention made of the Rectory of Bishopwearmouth which belonged to the Rector and was originally created out of the rectorial glebe. Another omission in the survey is the mention of free tenants. The nature of the book would lead us to expect this omission, for it is not so much an enumeration of all the holders of the land under the See, as of the services and customs due from the land; and as free tenants rendered nothing of that kind, they do not come into consideration in such a record as we have in Pudsey's survey.

Boldon Book may be called the Domesday Book of the County of Durham. It is impossible to over-rate its importance to the historical student, whether he be interested in the nature of the early tenures, the descent of property, or the social condition of the tenants. When this book was compiled our district consisted of moorland and extensive woods, with large open pastures and cultivated fields (without hedges or any divisions), near to the three little villages which now form the town of Sunderland. Each village had its herd for looking after the cattle, its pounder for taking care of stray cattle, and its smith and carpenter. All the inhabitants, except the free tenants, were the servants of the lord, and in return for the work they rendered him, they had each a portion of land which provided for the daily wants of the family.

Pudsey was Bishop of Durham for forty years, during the reigns of Stephen, Henry II., and Richard I.

He took a great interest in the Crusade, and in 1189 when Richard I. was selling honours and offices to raise money to join the Crusaders the Bishop was extorting money from his subjects for the same object.

With the large sums of money he obtained he is said to have built several vessels at Sunderland and Stockton to convey troops to Palestine.

Our local crusaders, under the Baron of Hylton, sailed from Hartlepool, then the chief seaport in the county. It may also be mentioned here that in 1347, five ships, with a hundred and forty-five men from the county, sailed from Hartlepool and took part in the siege of Calais.

Grant of Charter by Henry III. AN important and valuable charter was granted to our town by Henry III., in 1247. By this charter permission was given to establish a Merchants' guild, and the burgesses could buy and sell whatever merchandise they thought fit, without the payment of tolls, not only in Sunderland but also in any other free boroughs in the kingdom.

Particulars of our town under the Norman, Plantagenet, and other kings may be obtained from the successive leases of the borough granted by the Bishops of Durham to the Hedworth, Bertram, Bowes, Lambton and Ettrick families, but these were not calculated to develop local building, industry, and trade; and it was not until the Bishop's powers were curtailed by Henry VIII. that our port became of great importance.

GRANT OF CHARTER BY HENRY III.

In 1358 Bishop Hatfield leased the Borough of Sunderland to Richard Hedworth, of Southwick, for twenty years at a rent of £20 a year.

In 1390 Bishop Skirlaw granted a commission of survey of the river Wear.

In 1406 and 1418 the rents of the Borough of Sunderland, the ferryboats, fisheries, and the profits and duties accruing from ships, etc., plying to the port were accounted for to Cardinal Bishop Langley's auditor and chancellor.

In 1464 the Borough with the ferries and fisheries was leased to Robert Bertram.

About two hundred years after the Boldon Book had been compiled a survey of the county was made by Bishop Hatfield, and at this period Thomas Menville, the second son of John Fitz-Adam Menville, Lord of Howden, held the Borough with free rents worth thirty-two shillings and eightpence, the fisheries in the Wear, the Borough Court, the tolls, and the stallage with eight yares* belonging to the bishop; eight shillings rent from the prior of Durham for Ebyare, and eight shillings from John Hedworth for his yare, called Owen's yare, and the right of drawing a net in the harbour of the said Borough.

At the same time Thomas Menville also occupied Hynden (Hendon) for the building of vessels and paid two shillings annually to the Bishop. John Hobson held ten acres of the demesne, and paid eighteen shillings and fourpence annually. William Gray and sixteen other tenants held a hundred and forty acres, under certain rents in proportion to the tenure; and Robert

* A yare was a dam thrown across a river to impede the free run of the salmon, and so force them through the lock or trap in which they were taken.

Carter held an acre called Foreland and paid two shillings.

In addition to paying rent for use of part of the demesne John Hobson, William Gray and six other tenants also occupied portions of land as bond tenants and instead of working for the lord of the manor they made an annual payment of rent. The ten cottagers who occupied a total of eighty-four acres made a small payment of money, and at Christmas and Easter each made a payment of eight hens and forty eggs.

It is important to notice that during the period which had elapsed between the two surveys many of the personal services of the tenants had been commuted for money payments as rents.

Under the Plantagenet kings the Saxons and Normans practically became one people, and the use of English took the place of the Norman-French language in the Courts of Law.

After the loss of Normandy the Norman baron came to look on England as his home, his retainers married the daughters of the Saxon farmers, side by side Norman men-at-arms and Saxon peasants shed their blood in resistance to the tyranny of unjust kings or on the burning plains of Palestine; racial division and bitterness passed away, and all alike came to glory in the name of Englishmen.

Sunderland in Plantagenet Times BEFORE concluding this chapter let us try to describe the town as it appeared four hundred and thirty-two years ago. The three Wearmouths (for Sunderland was often called Wearmouth) were then small country villages. Most of the houses were single room dwellings, although these were gradually giving place to houses built of stone and covered with thatch or red tiles, and having an upper room called a solar.

The only large buildings in the district were the church, rectory, and tithe barns at Bishopwearmouth; the church at Monkwearmouth; and a few warehouses and toll houses at Wearmouth. Special features would be the large number of beautiful trees and the three manor mills.

It is impossible to give an accurate estimate of the number of inhabitants, but when we consider that in 1681 there were less than 3,000 people living in this locality we feel justified in stating that the population in 1486 would not exceed 1,000.

While the town was slowly increasing in size, the trading burgesses were becoming enriched under the charters and privileges granted to them.

Coal Staithes for loading keels were erected on both banks of the river and the town was becoming known for its shipbuilding.

At regular intervals agricultural produce and cattle were brought from outlying districts and sold in the town.

Honey, in those days used instead of sugar, and salt obtained from sea water, were plentiful and there were large quantities of salmon and other fish. A much larger proportion of fish was eaten then than now, as it took the place of flesh meat during days of abstinence.

Bread and ale, the chief articles of food and drink, were under the supervision of the Bishop's bailiff whose duty it was to protect the buyers from extortion and to see that the articles were of good quality and correct weight. Bishop Pudsey's Charter (Clause 15) shows that the seller was liable to fine or imprisonment if found guilty of charging too much or giving unjust weight.

A maximum price for the necessaries of life was fixed during the reign of Edward I. (1272 to 1307), and continued, with occasional modifications, for many years. In 1393 during the reign of Richard II., the last of the Plantagenet kings, the following prices of victuals and drink were proclaimed :—

	£	s.	d.
A carcase of choice beef	1	0	4
A carcase of hog	0	3	4
A carcase of veal	0	2	6
A carcase of mutton	0	1	8
A carcase of lamb	0	0	8
A fresh salmon, the largest and best	0	2	0
A fat goose	0	0	4
A hen	0	0	1
Good wheaten bread, for four loaves	0	0	1
Oats, per bushel	0	0	1½
Claret and red wine, per gallon	0	0	8
Strong beer, per gallon	0	0	1

The money then in use in our county consisted chiefly of silver pennies struck by the Bishops at their mint at Durham. Many of these coins are to be seen in our local museum. They differ from the ordinary coins of the realm on their reverse sides only, where they have inscriptions and initial letters to indicate in which Bishop's reign they were issued; those of Wolsey bearing, in addition, the Cardinal's hat. Bishop Tunstall, who succeeded Wolsey in 1539, was the last Bishop of Durham who had the privilege of coining. It is estimated that the value of a penny would be equal to two shillings and sixpence of our money before the war of 1914 to 1918.

Bishopwearmouth Rectory 1807.

CHAPTER V.

SUNDERLAND IN TUDOR AND STUART TIMES.
1485 TO 1714.

Sunderland prospered greatly under the Tudor sovereigns whose wise policy it was to create a strong fleet, to encourage the production of large supplies of home grown corn, and to be completely independent of the foreigner.

Queen Elizabeth's Commission of 1558
STATE regulations of trade and industry by means of what was known as the Mercantile System were introduced, and alien merchants were no longer encouraged to the detriment of the home trader. In carrying forward this policy, Queen Elizabeth, in 1558, appointed a Commission to inquire into the number of creeks belonging to the port of Newcastle. Five creeks were reported as belonging to Newcastle, viz. : Blythe, Sunderland, Hartlepool, Stockton, and Whitby. Hartlepool and Whitby were described as being most frequented for traffic, but that Hartlepool was much decayed and that the pier ought to be repaired. The other three creeks were said to be little frequented or haunted with traffic of merchants or merchandise. As a result of the Commissioners' report, Sunderland, for many years, was accounted a part or creek of the port of Newcastle !

The township of Wearmouth Panns derived its name from the ten salt pans (or panns) which are mentioned in the survey carried out by command of Elizabeth in 1587.

The old township extended along the south bank of the Wear from the bridge to Russell Street and had been gradually gained from the river by embankments. Messrs. Austin & Sons' shipyard now occupies the site of the ancient salt pans.

Between the years 1600 and 1630, a considerable number of Scottish families and foreign merchants settled in the town. This was not permitted in neighbouring towns where the powerful Trade Guilds prevented the settlement or employment of people from other parts.

In 1615 there was a general muster of all men fit to bear arms, within the Bishopric, between the ages of 16 and 60. The number of men present at this array, which was held on Spenny Moor, near Whitworth, amounted to 8,320. Sunderland and Bishopwearmouth furnished 196 men and Monkwearmouth 87.

Bishop Morton's Charter, 1634 SUNDERLAND had been hitherto governed by a bailiff appointed by the Bishop, but in the year 1634, Bishop Morton, to encourage the increasing trade of the port, incorporated the burgesses and inhabitants by the title of Mayor, twelve Aldermen, and Commonalty of the Borough of Sunderland.

The charter states that Sunderland had beyond the memory of man, been an ancient borough, known by the name of the New Borough of Wearmouth, containing in itself a certain port where ships had plied, bringing and carrying merchandise, as well as to and from certain other ports of the kingdom ; the articles herein specified are sea coals, grindstones, rubstones, and whetstones.

It also states that the trade was then greatly increased,

by reason of the multitude of ships that resorted thither; and the borough had anciently enjoyed divers liberties and free customs, as well by prescription, as by virtue of sundry charters from the Bishops of Durham, confirmed to them by the crown ; which from defect in form, proved insufficient for the support of the ancient liberties, privileges, and free customs of the borough.

The corporation was empowered by the charter to hold lands, to have a common seal, and to have one court, to be holden one day every three weeks, before their recorder. At this court, actions, suits, quarrels, and debts not exceeding £40, might be tried ; and its sergeants were empowered to execute its warrants, distresses, attachments, and other precepts.

The gentlemen incorporated under the charter were as follows :—

MAYOR.
Sir William Belasyse, of Morton House,
(High Sheriff of Durham)

ALDERMEN.
Sir William Lambton, of Lambton.
Thomas Wharton, of Winston, Esquire.
Hugh Wright, of Durham, Esquire.
Robert Bowes, of Biddic-Waterville, Esquire.
Hugh Walton, Alderman, of Durham.
George Gray, of Southwick, Gentleman.
Francis James, of Hetton, Esquire.
Richard Hedworth, of Chester Deanery, Esquire.
William Langley, of Stainton, Esquire.
George Lilburne, of Sunderland, Gentleman.
George Burgorn, of Wearmouth, Gentleman.
George Walton, Alderman of Durham.

Common Council Men.

William Wycliffe.	Edward Lee.
William Freeman.	John Harrison.
Thomas Snowdon.	Adam Burdon.
Thomas Atkinson.	William Caldwell.
Thomas Lacie.	Robert Young.
William Potts.	Robert Collingwood.
William Thompson	Clement Oldcorn.
Thomas Scarborough.	Humphrey Harrison.
John Husband.	Christopher Dickenson.
George Humble.	William Watt.
John Hardcastle.	William Dossey.
William Huntley.	Thomas Palmer.

Recorder.

John Richardson, of Durham, Esquire.
(Solicitor-General to Bishops Morton and James)

The Corporation was to have power to make laws for the regulation of the borough and its trade. The markets were to be held every Friday; and there were to be two fairs, or marts, held every year in May and October. (The last Sunderland fair was held on the 13th and 14th of October, 1868.)

Notwithstanding the advantages and importance conferred on the town by this charter, it was allowed to fall into disuse; no election having been held to replace the corporation officials appointed by the Bishop. Probably this may have arisen from the uncertainty and distrust which preceeded the civil war. Although the members of the corporation did not preserve their jurisdiction, the privileges granted to the town under this charter have been expressly acknowledged by the crown and law courts.

THE CIVIL WAR

It may be mentioned here that the tax known as ship money was first levied in the year after this charter was granted, and that the ports of Sunderland, Hartlepool, and Stockton were charged with one ship of the burthen of 200 tons for the services of the state, manned with eighty men, and double equipage, with ammunition, wages, and victuals, at the expense of £1850, levied by a rate of 3/6 in the pound.

At this period our town was held under two leases granted by the Bishop. The lease including the borough, the courts, fairs, markets, tolls, anchorage and beaconage, was vested in the Lambton family; and the other, comprising the ferry-boats, the metage, and tolls of fruit, herbs, and roots, was held by the family of Ettrick. The lease of the ferries was purchased by the Commissioners of the Wearmouth Bridge in 1795.

The Civil War WE have now reached that period in the history of the town when the war between Charles I. and the Parliament commenced. Sunderland then became a place of considerable consequence, not so much from its positive importance, as from the circumstance that Newcastle, from 1642 to 1644, was stoutly and loyally defended for the king, and in consequence the export of coal from Newcastle was closed against the rebellious city of London. Under these circumstances, the collieries on the Wear, and the port of Sunderland, became of vital importance to the Parliamentary party, and the latter in 1642, established a garrison at Sunderland and appointed Sir William Armyne, one of the Parliamentary Commissioners, to reside in the town during the civil war.

Several of the most ancient and opulent families of the nobility and gentry of our district took part in the war on the side of the king. Amongst these were :—Sir William Lambton, one of the aldermen of Sunderland under Bishop Morton's charter, who fell at Marston Moor, on 2nd July, 1644; the two sons of Sir William Belasyse, the first mayor of Sunderland, who fell at Naseby; Colonel John Hylton and his son Captain Hylton, of Hylton Castle. On the Parliamentary side were Sir Henry Vane; Captain Robert Hutton, of Houghton; Captain Edward Shipperdson, of Morton; Captain Adam Shipperdson, of Bainbridge Holme; Nicholas Heath, of Little Eden; Thomas Shadforth, of Eppleton; Alderman George Gray, of Southwick; Captain Sharp, of Hawthorn; Alderman George Lilburne. Lieutenant-Colonel John Lilburn, Robert Lilburn, and many others. During the civil war George Lilburne was the only acting civil magistrate within the borough and it was greatly due to his influence that the town supported the Parliament during the unhappy contest. On the 2nd March, 1644, the Scottish Army, under the command of Alexander Leslie, Earl of Leven, entered Sunderland without any opposition, and encamped* on the open ground between Bishopwearmouth and Sunderland.

The river Wear, with its high precipitous cliffs, formed an impregnable defence on the north side of the camp, the other sides being protected by two trenches and mounds of earth, called the big dyke and the little dyke; in addition to these, forts and redoubts were erected; the place where the fort commanding the Pan ferry was situated is still known in the locality as "Carty Barty" i.e. Carter's Battery.

* The site of the camp was visible in the west Pann field until 1795 when the ground was levelled and built on.

Secure from the attacks of the king's party, the Scottish soldiers, when free from duty, wandered safely up and down the shady country lane between the little towns of Bishopwearmouth and Sunderland, and not a few visited the Rose and Crown Inn, built in 1615, to drink "success to the blue bonnets." Others would patronise the Red Lion Inn, erected in 1630, in Crowtree Road, then a charming lane with its high trees and noisy rookery. The church belfrey at Bishopwearmouth proved a convenient watch tower from which the sentry could descry any foraging party of the enemy operating in the neighbourhond.

The first conflict between the two parties took place about two and half miles west of Sunderland. The Scots being much provoked to come out of the town marched out in order of battle, but when they met the foe they were forced back into their trenches. Next morning they returned in greater numbers and attacked the rear of the Marquis of Newcastle's force and so disordered it that the whole of the royalist army was, for a time, in considerable danger, but Sir Charles Lucas who was then in command of the right wing, hastened to the rear, and with his regiment fell upon the Scots who were compelled to retire to their camp. The royalists then returned to Durham.

The large field at the west of Hylton Road, through which a footpath runs to Offerton, is pointed out as the scene of this conflict. The field is still known as the "battle-field" and the remains of trenches on the high ground at the south are locally known as the rifle pits.

On the 13th of March, the Scots, leaving two regiments to guard Sunderland, marched towards Durham but being unable to obtain forage for their horses they returned, crossed the Wear, and encamped near South Shields. The fort at South Shields, held for the king, was besieged and eventually taken on 20th March. Three days after this event the royalists, under the Marquis, were drawn up on the high ground near Hylton, on the north side of the river.

The Scots moved to meet them and selected the raised ground between Hylton and the sea as a favourable place for an engagement with the foe.

The seamen of our port brought one of the large guns from the Scots' camp and this together with a number of small field pieces formed the artillery of the Parliamentary side.

(It is said that a second large gun was lost in the river at this time. It was recovered 250 years afterwards and placed in the Barnes Park, where it may be seen, with this incription :—

"County Borough of Sunderland 1909

Dredged from the river Wear near the spot where the Scottish army of General Leslie crossed after having abandoned the siege of Newcastle-on-Tyne, in February 1644, when his soldiers camped in the Panns Field Sunderland, March 4th 1644").

The Armies faced one another all day on the 24th March, and towards night the cannon began to play, and parties of musqueteers endeavoured to drive one another from their hedges. The field word, given by the Marquis to his troops, was *"Now or Never."*

The Scots charged shouting—"The Lord of hosts is with us." Many were slain on each side but no decisive victory was gained. The troops continued to face each other the following day, when the Marquis seeing no probability of bringing the Scots to engage again, retired towards Durham. A party of Scottish horse pursued and a smart skirmish took place with the rear guards until Lucas's brigade repulsed the enemy. On the retreat of the royalists the Scots marched to Easington, where they remained until the 8th April and then marched to Quarrington Hill from whence they joined the Parliamentary forces under Fairfax, at Tadcaster, on 20th April, 1644. The Marquis of Newcastle and his forces were then at York.

No other engagements took place in our district with the exception of small skirmishes between the foraging parties of each side.

The fatal battle of Marston Moor, on 2nd July, 1644, completed the ruin of the king's affairs in the north, and was soon followed by the surrender of York. Newcastle, the last bulwark of the royal cause in the north, was taken by storm, after a most gallant defence, on the 19th October, 1644, and three years afterwards the Scottish army was withdrawn from England and disbanded. There were many conflicts at sea, during this period, and many Sunderland vessels were captured. The ships of the Parliamentary party were under the command of the Earl of Warwick and the wooden walls of Old England performed most effective service. In March, 1644, the "Endeavour" and three other of the king's ships were captured off Sunderland, and in July of the same year a ship, loaded with ammunition, small arms, and twenty-two pieces of ordnance for Newcastle, was captured and brought into our port.

The royalists were equally active at sea, under Sir Hugh Cholmey, and succeeded in capturing a total of forty Sunderland vessels, on their passage to London with coals.

The Scots, when encamped at Sunderland, received supplies by sea from Scotland but frequently their ships were wrecked or taken by the enemy. On one occasion when five ships sailed from Scotland three were lost during a severe storm and the other two were driven into the Tyne by the extremity of the weather and seized by the royalists.

On the 11th March, 1644 two ships arrived safely from Scotland, and one with supplies of cheese and butter from London.

Tragedy on the Town Moor As the Scots were frequently short of provisions, foraging parties of horse soldiers, were appointed to visit the farms in the neighbourhood of our town. When any cattle, horses, or hay were taken, the farmer was given a draft on the Parliamentary Commissioners in payment.

Local tradition states that Captain Dalrymple and a party of soldiers paid a visit to Luke Lawson, the hind, who occupied a small farm on the Sunderland Town Moor.

The Captain arranged to take four stacks of hay, three cows, and two horses and offered a draft of £22 in payment. Luke, however, refused to accept less than £43 and seeing his cattle driven away by the soldiers, he, in a moment of anger and excitement, rushed into his house, seized his gun and returning shot Captain Dalrymple.

The sergeant of the troops hearing the report, and seeing his Captain fall dead, immediately ordered his men to fire. Luke was killed and unfortunately, just as the men fired, Mrs Lawson and her daughter Mary ran towards Luke and when the smoke cleared away it was seen that they too, had fallen victims to the ruthlessness of war.

A military investigation absolved the sergeant from any blame for his hasty order.

Tragedy at Bishopwearmouth ANOTHER tragedy is said to have occurred at Bishopwearmouth about the same period. In one of the small houses, situated at the south east of the rectory grounds, lived an elderly man who was supposed to be very wealthy ; it was said he kept his money in a strong oak box. One day he was missing and his residence was found to have been broken into and plundered, but the mystery was never solved until 1902 when some of the ancient dwellings were pulled down to make room for a new fire station. Several labourers engaged in digging for the foundations of the new building discovered an oak box containing from three hundred to four hundred silver coins, chiefly groats, sixpences, and shillings of the reigns of Mary, Elizabeth, James, and Charles 1. Those who obtained the largest share of this "treasure trove" threw down their tools, left their work and never returned. A few days afterwards, the workmen discovered the skeleton of a man, but the bones crumbled away when exposed to the air. Possibly the old man had hidden his money underground before he was slain and buried by his murderers.

The builder of the new premises managed to purchase a few of the coins and had them enclosed in neat leather cases as mementoes for presentation to the members of the building committee.

Notwithstanding that Sunderland passed so ingloriously into the hands of the Parliamentary party, without so much as as single blow being struck, there still remained in the town many sympathisers with the unfortunate Charles 1, and a plot was formed to seize the town for the King. The seamen of the port, however, obtained arms and two pieces of ordnance and thereby defeated the plans of the King's supporters. For their prompt action Parliament awarded the sum of two hundred pounds to the seamen.

The whole of Durham came entirely under the power of the Parliamentary party and was governed by Sir William Armyne and other commissioners during the protectorate of Oliver Cromwell.

Bishop-wearmouth Rectory THE old rectory and out buildings have already been mentioned (chapter 2) and as the ancient mansion house was considerably damaged during the civil war further particulars are now given. The rectory house and grounds were situated at the north of the church, from which they were separated by the western end of High Street. They occupied the site of a very ancient religious house of the monastic class. A memorandum, dated 29th August, 1650 states that "whereas the parsonage-house at Bishopwearmouth was in the year 1646 defaced and exceedingly ruined by armies, the Rev. William Johnson, admitted at that time to the rectory, had since disbursed considerable sums of money to make the same habitable: in all £41-8-0." After the restoration of Charles 2, the south part of the rectory was partly rebuilt by the Rev. R. Grey, and finished by his successor, the Rev. Dr. Smith, whose arms were placed on the south front. He received £100 for dilapidations and expended £600 on the house.

The Park was enclosed from the adjoining gill by the Rev. H. Egerton (brother of Bishop Egerton) who became rector of the parish in 1776. The last rector who occupied the rectory was the Hon. and Rev. Gerard

Vallerian Wellesley (brother of the Duke of Wellington) who was appointed in 1827, and lived here in sumptuous style.

In 1855 the rectory, with its outbuildings and grounds was sold; the house was demolished and the land, comprising an area of nearly three acres, built upon. The Rectory Park Schools occupy the western portion of the park, close to the site of the old parsonage. The fine old Norman doorway and the iron-studded oak door, which formed the southern entrance to the courtyard of the rectory house were carefully preserved when the building was taken down, and presented to the Sunderland Corporation who have fitly preserved the interesting relics in the Mowbray Park, where, at the foot of Building hill they form the entrance to the cave, cut out of the rock, which is used as a tool house by the park gardeners. The beautiful staircase of dark oak, with spirally-twisted balustrades of sixteenth century workmanship, was removed to the new rectory in Gray Road.*

Monk-wear-mouth Estates THERE are but few events of historical importance connected with Monkwearmouth during this period. After the monasteries were suppressed by King Henry the Eighth, in 1545, the monastic buildings and land at Monkwearmouth were granted to Thomas Whytehead. In 1597 these were conveyed to John Widdrington and in 1642 they became the property of Colonel George Fenwick, an active officer of the Parliamentary party. In 1646 Colonel Fenwick purchased from Parliament the Bishop's manor of Houghton-le-Spring and the borough of Sunderland for £2851-9-6 but at the

* The present rectory is situated at West Lodge, Tunstall Road.

restoration the latter reverted to the See. When Colonel Fenwick died he left two daughters : the elder married the celebrated parliamentary leader Sir Arthur Haslerigg, and the younger daughter, Dorothy, became the wife of Sir Thomas Williamson, the heir of Sir Thomas Williamson of Great Markham, Nottingham, a loyalist who had lost £30,000 in the cause of Charles I.

Lady Williamson, in 1689, purchased the Monkwearmouth estates from her nephew Sir Thomas Haslerigg, and left the estates to her husband. Members of the Williamson family of Monkwearmouth and Whitburn were High Sheriffs of Durham from 1723 until 1810. Sir Hedworth Williamson the seventh baronet, was Member of Parliament for the County in 1831, High Sheriff in 1840, and Member of Parliament for Sunderland in 1847.

Oaths of Supremacy and Obedience SHORTLY after the restoration of Charles II, that monarch directed his commission to the Mayor and four senior aldermen of the borough and to Walter Ettrick, Esquire, his majesty's officer of the customs to administer the oaths of supremacy and obedience to the inhabitants of our town.

Every school-boy has read about the great plague of London but it is not generally known that in the year 1665 the dreadful disease was imported to Sunderland by shipping, as appears from the following entry taken from the old register book of the parish of Bishopwearmouth, "Jeremy Reed, of Billingham, Kent, bringer of the plague of which died thirty persons out of Sunderland in three months, was buried on 5th July, 1665."

The Pier of 1669   IN the year 1669, Charles II granted letters patent to Edward Andrews, Esquire, empowering him to build a pier at Sunderland, to erect lighthouses, and to forbid the casting of ballast at sea within certain limits. He was also directed to cleanse the harbour from shoals and sandbanks, and powers were granted to him to levy contributions for these purposes, by a tonnage duty on ships frequenting the port. It is said that a pier was erected by Andrews but there are no documents or information to be obtained respecting it.

Local records and old plans of the harbour and river show that in 1706 much needed to be done to improve the port. The quay on the south side of the river then terminated a little way below the custom house; the banks of the river eastward then formed the northern boundary of the town moor. The high water mark on the north side of the river at this period, approached within 150 yards of the south end of Monkwearmouth Church: consequently a great portion of what is now dry land and formed into streets and shipyards was then overflowed by the tide. Numerous rocks and sand banks diverted the channel and the harbour was in an unprotected state, beacons being the only marks for the guidance of vessels entering and departing from the port. In a storm, therefore, no ship could safely attempt to take refuge in a harbour so exposed, with dangerous rocks at the entrance of its tortuous channel.

The increasing importance of Sunderland as a place of trade was viewed with extreme jealousy by the Corporation of Newcastle and when a proposal was submitted to Parliament, in 1706, for the improvement of the Wear, it was opposed by the Master and Brethern of

Newcastle Trinity House. Ten years afterwards when a Bill for the same purpose was introduced the corporation of Newcastle petitioned against it. How our port was improved until it became the safest on the north east coast will be told in the next chapter.

Sir Ambrose Crowley THE great increase of the coal trade during the reign of the Stuart kings brought prosperity to the town and amongst the many who were attracted to Sunderland for the purpose of trade mention must be made of Sir Ambrose Crowley, who, about the year 1682, erected works in Low Street for the manufacture of all kinds of iron goods including chains, edged-tools, files, hammers, locks, nails, and every sort of smith's ware. It appears that many of his workmen were foreigners and Catholics and they did not altogether meet with a friendly reception. For some reason the "Cyclopean Colony" as it was called, was transferred to the Tyne, in 1690, where the works continued until 1872. Sir Ambrose Crowley, who enjoyed the triple honours of Sheriff of London, Alderman of the city, and Member of Parliament for Andover, died in 1713 leaving large estates and £200,000 besides his factory at Tyneside.

Social conditions in Sunderland during the 17th Century TRADE and agriculture made great headway and there was plenty of work in the town and district. The wages of the peasant class rose to 6/- per week, with extra payment during the hay and corn harvests. The peasants wore breeches of strong woollen cloth or leather, worsted stockings, strong shoes and broad brimmed hats. Additional employment was provided for them by the introduction of turnips and other root crops from Holland. These proved a great boon for it then became possible to keep oxen throughout the winter, with the result of great benefit to the health of the people, who were no longer compelled to subsist almost entirely on salt meats.

The artisan or craftsman earned 9/- weekly. In summer he commenced work at five o'clock in the morning and worked until half past seven in the evening, with an interval of two and a half hours allowed for meals. From September to March he worked from daylight until it was dark, and if he absented himself from his work he was fined a penny per hour. The housewife was fully occupied in baking, cooking, brewing, spinning, and sewing for the members of the family. Food and clothing were much dearer than at the present time.* To express the cost in our money to day we should say that sugar was 2/- a pound, rice 2/4, bacon 2/4, candles 1/8, butter 2/8, and a leg of mutton 10/-. Linen was 8/- a yard, stockings 8/- a pair and shoes 12/-. Wooden platters were used as plates, and pewter pots and candle sticks were in common use. Home brewed beer took the place of tea, coffee, and cocoa which were then unknown.

During holidays there was dancing on the village green at Bishopwearmouth; shooting at the butts; wrestling; football and other games. Our local parish registers record that Richard Watson, who was killed at Sunderland whilst playing at football was buried on 15th January, 1667.

In Queen Elizabeth's days archery was being superseded by the gun, the use of which was encouraged in all towns and villages.

Fishing and shooting were common pastimes with Sunderland people whilst the cruel and degrading sports

* Pre-war time is meant.

of bull-baiting and cock fighting were favourite amusements of the day, not only in our town but practically in all parts of England. The ancient rolls of the Court Baron for the year 1681 record that Anthony Hodgson and other butchers of our town were each fined £1-19-11 (the highest fine the court could impose) for selling their bulls unbaited, to the damage of the liege people and against the forms of the statute. The various forms of legal punishment inflicted during this period are described in chapter eight.

In this stirring period, then, we see Sunderland gradually rising from the state of an obscure village to the dignity and importance of a busy sea-port town. And although its position prevented it from playing a very prominent part in the Great Civil War, yet the clash of arms was often heard within its borders and local men in the great conflict played a part which must be of deep historic interest to all Sunderland people who love the memory of brave deeds.

CHAPTER VI.

HANOVERIAN PERIOD, PART I.

The Piers, Light-houses, and Docks THE preservation and improvement of our port and river may be said to commence with the appointment of the River Wear Commissioners in the year 1717. The limits within which the Commissioners were then empowered to act extended from Souter Point on the North, to Ryhope Dene on the South, and Eastward into the sea to a depth of five fathoms at low water; they also had control of the river as far as Durham. A large and

Sunderland Church
(Consecrated in 1719)

THE PIERS, LIGHTHOUSES AND DOCKS 71

interesting volume could be written dealing with the work of the Commissioners and their eminent engineers during the past 200 years.

The results of their labours, during this period, may be seen in the magnificent piers, lighthouses, docks, warehouses, quays, and appliances for loading and discharging vessels of all sizes, but more wonderful than these monuments of skill and industry is the great change which has taken place in the river; enormous rocks and sandbanks have been removed; land has also been reclaimed on both banks; it has been widened in places and thousands of tons of river substance have been dredged annually from its bed, so that vessels of the largest size may enter or leave the port at any period of the tide.

Previous to 1717 the river and harbour were stated to be "very much gorged, stopped up, and choaked by many sholes, sand banks, and much breach and rubbish daily increasing in the same, almost rendered innavigable," and that "ships of small draught which may go into the said harbour, do lye long there for their loading by reason of the said sholes and sand banks obstructing the bringing down of coles &c for their loadings, and being so loaded do wait long for spring tydes and winds to carry them to sea."

One considerable object of attention under all the Acts passed since 1717, in connection with our port, was the building of the Piers, and from a statement printed in 1765 it appears that £50,000 had been then expended on the South Pier and it was still not completed.

This structure was exceedingly damaged by a high flood in November, 1771, and it was necessary to take it partly down and rebuild it in a different direction, where it would be less exposed to the violence of the sea and of land floods. The memorable flood of the 17th of November, 1771 inundated three collieries and destroyed three bridges on the Wear, as well as the old bridge at Newcastle, and caused great destruction of life and property at Sunderland. A number of keels and ships were driven from their moorings and carried away by the force of the flood. Part of the pier was carried away, and much damaged by the ships driving against it. It is said that thirty-four ships were wrecked at the mouth of the Wear during the flood.

The lighthouses erected on the South Pier were very interesting. The first, like the first Eddystone Lighthouse, was built of wood. There is an old French print of this ancient Sunderland lighthouse in the library collection of local prints and it depicts the lighthouse with two signboards attached, one with the words "Sail Maker" and the other "Good Wines for Sale."

It seems probable that while the upper part was used as a lighthouse the lower rooms were occupied respectively by a Sail Maker and a Wine Merchant.

In 1856 the old lighthouse, which stood at the eastern extremity of the South Pier, was taken down and replaced by an iron structure of loftier altitude, designed by Mr. Meek, Engineer to the R.W.C. and this is still standing. The old South Pier has always been a favourite promenade for the people of Sunderland. The view from its extremity extends from Souter Point, on the north, to the Cleveland Hills on the south, comprising a wide stretch of coast, in which the town of Hartlepool, twenty miles distant, can be easily seen on a clear day.

A start was made with the North Pier in 1787 and when it was completed in 1802, an elegant octagonal lighthouse, of stone, was built near the extremity from a design by Mr. Pickernell, Engineer. In 1841 when this pier had been extended the lighthouse was moved in an entire state, a distance of 450 feet, a very wonderful engineering feat for those days.

The following incription was cut on one of the stones of the lighthouse :—

> "This Lighthouse was built in 1802.
> JONATHAN PICKERNELL, Engineer.
> In the year 1841 it was removed in an entire state from its original site, a distance of 450 feet; gross weight 338 tons. JOHN MURRAY, Engineer."

After guiding the storm-tossed mariners for a hundred years this beautiful lighthouse was taken down, as the foundations of the old pier would no longer stand the weight, and a smaller one was erected in its plaee.

We trust that at some period the ancient lighthouse will be re-erected in one of our public parks as a monument to the genius of Messrs Pickernell and Murray and as an example of the skill and industry of British workmen of the past.

Roker Pier and Light-house THE pleasant sea-side resort of Roker owes much of its attractiveness to its magnificent pier and lighthouse. The pier is 2041 feet long, and stands ten feet above high water mark. The structure terminates with a round head on which is erected the attractive looking lighthouse, built of red and grey granite.

The lighthouse is a hundred and fifty feet in height and contains a brilliant revolving light of 45,000 candle power, and a powerful fog horn. The total cost of pier and lighthouse was nearly £300,000. The last stone used in the construction of this immense breakwater bears the inscription :—

"The foundation stone of the pier was laid on the 14th of September, 1885, by James Laing, Esquire, Chairman of the R.W.C. To record its completion this stone was placed in position on the 23rd of September, 1903, by the Right Honourable the Earl of Durham, Lord Lieutenant of the County;

Jenneson Taylor, Chairman to the Commissioners; Henry Hay Wake, M.I.C.E. Engineer."

Sunderland Docks THE Port of Sunderland extends from the Harbour entrance to Biddick ford, about eight miles from the mouth of the Wear. In connection with the port there are four large docks. The north dock belongs to the North Eastern Railway Company, and the three large docks on the south side of the river are the property of the Commissioners.

The foundation stone of the south dock was laid by Mr. Hudson, in the presence of an immense concourse of spectators, on the fourth of February, 1848, and the dock was formally opened on the 20th of June, 1850. At that date it enclosed eighteen and a half acres and it was estimated to accommodate 260 vessels, while the half tide basin would accommodate 38.

On the 24th of November, 1850, a second extension was completed and by this addition the dimensions of the docks were increased to thirty-two acres. In February, 1856, the southern half-tide basin and the sea outlet were finished, together with the tidal harbour, which had been enclosed from the sea. This portion of the works was opened on the 5th of March, 1856, when four gun boats, built on the Wear, proceeded to sea by the new outlet, the Mayor, A. J. Moore, Esq.: steering the first vessel.

The cost of the south docks up to this date was about £640,000 ; and the area enclosed for the tidal harbour, quays, warehouses, &c., was one hundred and twenty seven acres.

The Hendon Dock was next opened and the three docks now extend for more than a mile along the sea shore on the south of the river. The three docks are connected and there are two entrances, one direct from the sea and the other from the river.

As an indication of the vast extent of water enclosed by the two new piers, docks, and outlets, it may be mentioned that the area is equal to two hundred and ten acres.

The docks have extensive warehouse accommodation, and all the quays are furnished with hydraulic and steam cranes and other approved appliances for the rapid landing and shipping of cargoes of all kinds.

Sunderland has become one of the easiest and safest ports of access in Britain ; there are no dangers to navigation, and ships arrive in the heart of the commercial centre a few minutes after passing Roker Pier Lighthouse.

Trade of the Port SUNDERLAND is one of the largest coal shipping ports in the United Kingdom, the quantity of coal and coke shipped in 1904, was 5,117,230 tons. Even during the war, in 1914, 4,074,589 tons were exported.

There are twenty coal spouts, so arranged that a ship of three thousand tons can be loaded in a day, and it is estimated that 15,000 tons altogether can be shipped in one day.

Sunderland is also the largest iron ship-building port and there are works for the construction of marine engines, anchors, chains, ropes, and all kinds of articles required for ships. Into the port vessels bring timber, from all parts of the world ; iron ore, pig iron, esparto grass, and wood pulp, (for making paper), ice, tar, petroleum, hemp, chalk, building materials, grain, fruit, and potatoes ; while from the port vessels depart with cargoes of coal, coke, iron and steel rails, pig iron, machinery, fire bricks, cement, earthenware, lime, coal-tar, chemicals, bottles and glass, pitch, and creosote oil, &c.

The whole port is under the control and management of the River Wear Commissioners who are constantly striving to improve the trade and prosperity of our sea port.

Sunderland Life Boats   A natural sequence to the details of the Piers and Lighthouses is a short account of our local Life Boats, but first it will be necessary to make a few general observations respecting the first Life Boats.

It is impossible to assign to any one person the merit of inventing the Life boat.

Lionel Lukin, a London coachbuilder, took out the first patent for a life boat on the 2nd, November, 1785, and it may be claimed that his was the first " self righting " boat. The first Life boat was built at South Shields, by Mr. Greathead, in the year 1789, the inventor of this boat, which was "unsinkable" was William Wouldhave, the parish clerk of St. Hilda's Church in that town.

In 1850, the Duke of Northumberland, president of the National Life Boat Institution, offered a prize of 100 guineas for the best model of a lifeboat. No fewer than 280 plans and models were sent in to the committee of practical men, who were appointed to consider their merits. After the six models adjudged to be the best had been placed side by side and their points again carefully considered, the prize was awarded to Mr. James Beeching, of Great Yarmouth, whose boat was thought to possess the greatest number of good qualities. But although Mr. Beeching received the Duke's premium, the committee did not consider his boat, with all its merits, quite perfect.

Accordingly Mr. James Peake, Assistant Master Shipwright in the Royal Dockyard at Woolwich, assisted by Captain Washington, R.N., Hydrographer to the Admiralty, were requested to furnish a design for a lifeboat which should combine as many of the good points as possible of the best models submitted to the committee.

The boat they designed was built in Woolwich dockyard, and this boat, with even yet a few more improvements, is the model of the modern lifeboat.

The movement commenced by a few South Shields shipowners has developed into one of the most useful benevolent associations the world has ever seen—"The Royal National Lifeboat Institution"—whose boats are the means of saving thousands of lives every year. This society is entirely supported by voluntary contributions to its funds, and well deserves the continued and increasing support of the benevolent.

Turning now to our sea port we find that in the year 1799 a very valuable vessel was wrecked at the mouth of the harbour and this led to a public subscription for the purpose of having a life boat built and equipped to be permanently stationed at Sunderland. The first boat was constructed in 1800 on an original plan suggested by Mr. John Davison. Within this life boat were a large number of air-tight compartments, so that if the boat should be staved by striking a rock, only the broken compartments would admit the water. There were four apertures through the bottom of the boat that opened and discharged the water when the sea broke on board, closing again, when she was clear.

The seats in the centre were for the crew, and the shipwrecked men were accommodated at each end of the boat. The keel was shod with iron, which added to its strength and took the place of ballast. The only cork used was round the outside and this answered the purpose of a "fender" and also added to the buoyancy of the vessel. A brass wire went round the gunwale to prevent the men being washed out, and a rope on each side of the seats answered the same purpose for the rowers.

It was claimed for this boat, that when filled with water, and as many men as it could hold, it would still be sufficiently buoyant to preclude all danger of sinking.

In recognition of his valuable invention Mr. Davison was awarded the honorary medallion of the Royal Humane Society, which was handed to him by his Royal Highness, the Duke of Sussex, President of the Institution.

The second local life boat was built in 1808, and in 1858 a new life boat was presented to the port by Miss Burdett Coutts of London. In 1865 a very fine life boat, named the "Florence Nightingale," arrived at Sunderland from the Royal National Life Boat Institution.

In 1909 there were four life boats stationed here; one at the south outlet, one at the south pier, one at Roker, and one at Hendon. Three of these were withdrawn, leaving the "George Woofinden," stationed at Thornhill Quay.

SUNDERLAND LIFE BOATS

The Royal Lifeboat Institute is gradually withdrawing the ordinary lifeboats from service and replacing them by powerful motor boats. There are already 35 of these splendid boats in use and on the 20th February 1918 the fine motor lifeboat, the "Henry Vernon," which for some years had done excellent service off the Tyne, was transferred to Sunderland and the "George Woofinden" was withdrawn from the port. The new lifeboat, which carries a crew of 12, and is fitted with a strong petrol motor of 40 horse-power and develops a speed of 8¾ knot under normal conditions, will be a valuable acquisition to our port. The vessel has a splendid reputation. She is a grand sea boat and has been instrumental in rescuing 250 persons during the last six years. The boat was given by Mr. A. Vernon, of Weston-super-Mare to the Lifeboat Institution, and it will be permanently stationed at Sunderland. It was brought over from the Tyne under the command of Coxwain Thomas Davison and Mr. W. J. Oliver, the hon. secretary of the local life brigade. The vessel is stationed at the new lifeboat house opposite the R.W. Commissioners old office, near the north entrance to the South Docks. It will interest Sunderland people to know that the "Henry Vernon" rendered splendid war service in connection with the wreck of the hospital ship "Rohilla," which was wrecked on Friday, 30th October, 1914, at Whitby.

The Whitby lifeboat saved 35 lives from the vessel but was unfortunately rendered unfit for further service and so the "Henry Vernon" was summoned by telegram. After travelling 44 miles through the night and storm, unguided by any coast lights (which were all extinguished on account of the war) she was brought into Whitby harbour at 1 a.m. on Sunday. After a brief period of rest and preparation the boat left the harbour for the wreck, taking a supply of oil to subdue the waves. Handled with splendid skill and courage the boat, after great difficulty, rescued the 50 people on board the "Rohilla," who had survived the terrible ordeal for so many hours.

The crews of the Sunderland lifeboats have been the means of saving 250 lives. The members of the Sunderland Volunteer Life Brigade, organised by Captain Coulson, in 1879, hold the record for life saving by means of the rocket apparatus. They have been called into action on seventy three occasions and have landed 292 persons from stranded or wrecked vessels.

South Shields has done honour to the memory of Mr. Wouldhave and Mr. Greathead, by erecting a beautiful monument near Marine Park, and close at hand, protected trom the inclement weather by a shed, may be seen the old liteboat "Tyne," the second of the South Shields lifeboats. Built in 1833, and withdrawn from service in 1887, this famous boat, during the fifty four years service was instrumental in saving 1024 lives.

At some period of the history of our town a monument may be erected to the memory of John Davison, the inventor of the first Sunderland lifeboat and to Captain Coulson, the originator of the Rocket Apparatus at Sunderland.

Sunderland Bridge DURING the latter part of the eighteenth century, the mode of communication between Sunderland and Monkwearmouth, by means of the ferries, became extremely inconvenient and the delay and interruption to business were severely felt.

Under these circumstances Mr. Rowland Burdon, Member of Parliament for the County of Durham, proposed the erection of a bridge across the Wear, at Sunderland. An act of parliament was obtained in 1792, and the foundation stone was laid on 24th September, 1793.

The novelty and advantage of the plan adopted in building the bridge consisted in retaining the usual form and principle of the stone arch in the erection of a cast iron bridge.

This was done by the subdivison of the iron into separate frames answering to the keystones of a common arch, and which, with a much greater degree of lightness, possess, when brought to bear on each other, all the firmness and strength of the solid stone arch.

The whole weight of iron which forms this immense structure is only 250 tons. Mr. Robert Stephenson, Engineer, described this bridge as a "noble and splendid structure, which, for the extent of space, combined with the astonishingly small weight of iron employed on its structure, has no parallel in this or any other country." The bridge was completed within three years, under the able and zealous direction of Mr. Thomas Wilson, Architect, of Bishopwearmouth.

During the period of erection there was no interruption to the navigation of the river. The bridge was opened for general use, in the presence of His Royal Highness, the Duke of Gloucester, on the 9th of August, 1796, after a very splendid masonic ceremony. The number of spectators was computed at 80,000.

The whole expense of the erection, including every sum laid out on account of it was £41,300, of which £30,000 was subscribed by Mr. Burdon; the money thus

G

advanced was secured on tolls, with five per cent interest, and all accumulations were used in the repayment of the capital. On the 12th November, 1846, the bridge was made free of all toll for foot passengers; the tolls on vehicles and cattle being abolished on 9th of November, 1885. In 1858 it was found that the bridge was no longer suitable for the increased traffic, so it was re-modelled, improved, and widened at a cost of £40,000 in 1859. It is still the largest single arch cast-iron bridge in England, but the enormous increase of traffic across the bridge and the immense weight of materials crossing daily for use in shipyards, &c., render it necessary to again re-model it or erect a new one in its place.

The Railway Bridge A little to the west of the Sunderland bridge is the large iron bridge, built by the North Eastern Railway Company, in 1879.

Before this was constructed passengers to Newcastle and the north had to start from Monkwearmouth Station, and townspeople going to Durham and the south took their departure from the old railway station which stood in Burdon Road.

The Queen Alexandra Bridge THE most important event, for our town, in the year 1909, was the opening of the above bridge, connecting Sunderland and Southwick. The erection of this massive bridge was a remarkable engineering feat, the huge span of steel in the middle, 353¾ feet long, is the heaviest in Britain, and rests on massive granite piers 300 feet apart. It is practically a double bridge, and like the High Level Bridge, at Newcastle, the railway runs above that part of the bridge provided for foot passengers and vehicles.

It was designed by Mr. Harrison, Chief Engineer of the N.E.R. Company, and built by Sir William Arrol & Co., "the bridge builders of the world." The total cost was £450,000 and of this sum the Railway Co., provided £239,000 ; the Corporation of Sunderland £200,000 and the Southwick Urban Council £11,000.

The Earl of Durham, who performed the opening ceremony was presented with a medal, which had been struck in commemoration of the event.

Sunderland Parish Church

SUNDERLAND remained included in the Parish of Bishopwearmouth until the year 1719, when, on account of the increasing population of the place, an Act of Parliament was obtained for making Sunderland a distinct and separate Parish.

The preamble of the Act states that Bishopwearmouth Church was the only parochial structure, and was totally inadequate to contain, with other inhabitants of the Parish, the population of Sunderland, amounting to 6,000 souls and that the inhabitants had erected a handsome church and parsonage on a parcel of ground called the "Intack," within the Manor and Borough of Sunderland, and had a separate plot adjoining for a burial place.

Sunderland Church is a spacious building of brick, with a square tower ; the Nave has two regular aisles formed by pillars with Corinthian capitals ; the Altar stands in a circular recess, covered by a dome, and opening into the Nave with two fluted columns. The church was consecrated by the Bishop of London, on the 5th of September, 1719.

The Rev. Robert Gray, M.A., who was rector from 1819 until 1839, was mainly instrumental in the establishment of the Gray National Schools on the town moor.

Sunderland Churchyard contains the grave of Jack Crawford. On the monument is the following inscription:

<blockquote>
The Grave
of
JACK CRAWFORD,
The Hero of Camperdown,
The Sailor who heroically nailed Admiral Duncan's flag to the top-gallant mast of H.M.S. Venerable, After it had been shot away at the glorious action of Camperdown, October 11th, 1797.
Jack Crawford was born at the Pottery Bank, Sunderland, 1775.
And died in his native town, 1831, aged 55 years.
Erected by Public Subscription, 1888.
</blockquote>

Sunderland Town Moor

CENTURIES ago the moor was known as the "Coney Garth" and the "Coney Warren" and under these names it is mentioned in the ancient rolls of the Wearmouth monastery.

There is no doubt that the common pasturage confirmed by Bishop Pudsey's Charter of 1154 refers to the town moor. At that date it was bounded on the north by the river Wear; on the south by a small ravine, afterwards known as Robinson's dene; on the east by the North Sea; and on the west by land known as the great moor. In ancient times it was of vast extent and even in the 17th century it included about eighty acres of land. From time immemorial the town moor was appropriated for public convenience, recreation, and enjoyment. Amongst other uses may be mentioned:—

(1). The fishermen claimed the right, from ancient usages, of drying their nets upon it.

(2). The inhabitants generally used it for drying and bleaching their linen.

(3). It was used as a pasturage for cattle.

(4). It was a recognised place for sports, such as bowling, horse racing, bull-baiting, spel-an-ore, or buckstick, quoits, foot racing, football, cricket and other games.

(5). The large pond which was situated near the southern extremity was used as a watering place for horses, and by lads and young men for the navigation of their fleets of little vessels, many of which were neatly and correctly rigged. In winter, skating on the pond was a favourite pastime.

(6). It was the favourite meeting place for sailors and keelmen.

There are many interesting incidents connected with the moor. It was here that the early followers of The Wesleys held their meetings in Sunderland and it has been said that when Whitfield preached, at the north end of the moor, the people at Monkwearmouth Shore heard part of the sermon. On the moor the Primitive Methodists held their first camp meeting at Sunderland.

In the year 1718 the moor was divided by stone walls into three divisions known as, the Great Moor, the North Moor, and the Intake. It was on the Intake that Sunderland church was erected in 1719. St. John's Church was built in 1769 on ground which had once been part of the moor.

Forts and Batteries IN former days there were several forts and open batteries on the moor. The first was a battery of four guns, situated at the river entrance. The position of this, the most ancient battery on record in our district, was such as effectually commanded the "Stell," or north channel of the river, as well as the roadstead. This fort is shown on a plan of the moor made by Mr. Thomas Forster in 1742.

A second battery, also having four guns, was built at Jockey Dike Nook, on the moor, about the year 1745. It was washed away by the sea in 1780. Upon the sand thrown up behind the south pier was erected the enclosed battery known as the Black Cat Battery, or, as it was afterwards called, Paul Jones' Battery. In addition to a fourth battery, built in 1783, there were two platforms on the moor on which cannon were placed for the defence of the port. During the wars of the French Revolution two platforms, each having two large guns (24 pounders) were erected at Hendon. The words "Hendon Bay" were painted on the gun carriages.

Most of our local forts and batteries were washed away by the sea; indeed, the constant encroachments of the ocean are responsible for reducing the size of the town moor and it has been further reduced by the erection of barracks, forts, streets of houses, Hendon Lodge, Sunderland Church, Gray National Schools, Orphan Asylum Docks, and by the purchase of land by the N.E.R. Co., who have power to occupy further portions of the moor when needed.

The Spa Well   A plan of the river Wear, published in 1737, shows the site of the once famous Spa Well. This appears to have been in the zenith of its popularity during the 18th century. The medicinal waters issued from a spring in the bank and fell into a stone trough provided for the purpose.

A number of stone steps led down to the trough the whole being covered and protected by a brick arch, open to the eastward. The moor and well are frequently mentioned in ancient records; in the rolls of the court baron for 1681, it is stated, "That the Freemen and Stallingers, and Widows, having any interest in the town moor, do repair aud repave that part of High Street belonging to the town moor and common ground fold, within six months."

In the accounts kept by the Freeman and Stallingers, who had charge of the common pasturage of Sunderland, we find the following interesting items :—

1718. For repairing the Spa Well £2-0-6.
1720. To sending the bellman to forbid the bowlers 6d.
1722. Received from the booths on the moor £2-0-4 (probably during the fair).

The Spa Well was washed away by the sea early in the 19th century and the last record concerning it dates from July, 1849, when during the excavation of the South Dock, a spring of water, strongly impregnated with sulphur and saline substances was discovered gushing out of a rock at the bottom of the south east corner of the dock. This was identified as the spring which had supplied the old Spa Well.

There was also a lime kiln on the sea banks at the north east end of the moor and according to tradition a wind mill once stood near the north west boundary of the moor. Although its former beauty has departed, what remains of the moor still has its uses. It provides a large open space, in a very crowded district, and makes a suitable playground for the younger generation of the ancient parish of Sunderland-by-the-sea.

Sunderland as a Sea Side Resort It is difficult to imagine that less than a hundred years ago, old Sunderland had some claim to be regarded as a fashionable sea side resort. Numbers of people came from different parts of the county to partake of the waters of the spa and amongst those who regularly took up their abode in our town, during the bathing season, was the Countess of Darlington. In 1821 new bathing machines were established near the moor, and excellent hot water baths were erected. Hendon, too, had a good supply of sea bathing machines, and hot and cold salt water baths.

There was ample accommodation for visitors, in private houses, and at the Hendon Bath Hotel. The visitors would enjoy walking over the town moor and they could find shelter, from the heat of the sun, under the tall trees and hedges, and in the picturesque little ravines which led from the moor to the clean sandy beach.

Population and Growth of Sunderland

No difficulty is experienced in giving the population of Sunderland from the year 1801, but before that time, when calculations were based on information from parochial registers, introduced in 1538, and other records, only an approximation of the number of people residing in our town could be obtained. The following figures will indicate the increase of population, at certain intervals, during the last 438 years.

Year.	Population.	Authority.
1481	1300	
1681	3090	Hutchinson
1781	20,940	,,
1801	24,469	Corporation Year book
1851	64,720	,, ,,
1901	146,077	,, ,,
1911	151,159	,, ,,
1916	154,041	,, ,,
1917	148,278 *	,, ,,
1918	145,000 *	,, ,,

* Decrease due to men still in the Army and Navy.

It may be interesting to tabulate the chief causes of this rapid increase in the population and wonderful growth of the town during the last 200 years.

(1). The appointment of the River Wear Commissioners in 1717. This led to the improvement of the harbour, building of piers, &c., and opening of docks, in 1850.
(2). Erection of the Wearmouth Bridge in 1796.
(3). Opening of new collieries in the district.
(4). Introduction of steam power and railways.
(5). The facilities the town afforded for shipping trade.
(6). Increased importance of the town when made a Parliamentary Borough, in 1832.
(7), The incorporation of the Borough in 1836.
(8). Sunderland made a County Borough in 1888.
(9). The power acquired by the Town Council through Acts of Parliament.
(10). The reputation of Sunderland as a Ship building town.

In the history of the town there have been periods when work was plentiful and wages were high and these conditions caused an influx of people from other parts, chiefly country districts. During such times many new dwellings were erected and large sums of money spent on public buildings.

Between the year 1795 and 1829 the sum of £101,000 was spent on public edifices alone ; twelve new chapels and places of worship being erected at a cost of £30,000.

In 1821 the population of Sunderland formed one seventh of the population of the whole county. The eighty years between 1750 and 1830 were exceedingly prosperous, the number of ships belonging to the port ; the trade ; and the population ; are all said to have been doubled during this time.

A report printed by order of the House of Commons on 11th March, 1828, shows that Sunderland was then in point of maritime importance, the fourth port of the United Kingdom and that it had one twenty-first part of the tonnage of the United Kingdom, or one seventeenth of the whole tonnage of England.

Sunderland Street Names WHEN Sunderland was made a separate parish a busy time commenced for house builders. Moor Street and the east part of Coronation Street were erected in 1820, at the time of the Coronation of George IV., Spring Garden Lane, and Covent Garden Lane (in George III's time beautiful gardens), were built in 1822 and a few years afterwards Silver Street, Neasham Square and New Gray Street also took the place of fields and gardens.

Sunderland street names provide an interesting subject for all lovers of local history. One naturally finds many names of former well known landowners and prominent Sunderland people handed down to posterity in our Street names ; thus we have Ettrick Place, Lilburn Street, Pemberton Street, Hartley Street, Havelock Street, Burleigh Street, Maude's Lane, Stamp's Lane, Neasham's Square and Maling's Rigg, all in old Sunderland ; Lambton Street, Clanny Street, St. Bede's Terrace, Paley Street, Canon Cockin Street, Fenwick Street, Tatham Street, Fawcett Street, Ayres Quay, and Cowan Terrace, at Bishopwearmouth ; and Hedworth Street, Williamson Street, Victor Street, and Dame Dorothy Street, at Monkwearmouth.

In Sunderland, as in most other towns, the names of poets, statesmen, warriors, kings, queens, and princes have been freely requisitioned to bestow on streets, nor have we forgotten our naval and military heroes or the places where they won their laurels.

Some of our street names remind us of the local residences of former merchant princes of the town ; thus we have Cresswell Terrace, Lodge Terrace, Thornhill Crescent, White House Crescent, Grange Terrace, Fenwick Street, Frederick Street, and Vine Place.

Some of the old residences are still standing, though now without their former beauty.

St. George's Square, the Bede Secondary School, and Cowan Terrace Council School, have been erected on ground which formed part of the Grange Park ; Fenwick Street is built on the carriage drive which led to Fenwick Lodge ; Frederick Lodge is now very difficult to find as it is shut in by business premises and the Arcade stands on the site of its fine orchard. Vine Lodge, once the residence of a local shipowner, and named after one of his vessels, has been completely changed by erecting Olive House and the adjoining shops on the ground where stood the front flower garden and entrance gate.

Street names which remind us of bygone days are Warren Street, which denotes the site of a coney or rabbit warren that once existed at the east end of the town ; Bodlewell Lane and Water Lane from which the inhabitants of old Sunderland obtained their drinking water.

Mill Hill, Mill Lane, and Old Mill Road, which indicate the vicinity of ancient windmills ; and Ropery Lane, Ropery Walk, and Ropery Row, which were hives of industry in the old wooden ship days.

High Street HIGH Street was formerly an open road commencing near the Low Row. After passing the Church and Crowtree Lane, it proceeded nearly in a straight easterly direction. The road led through the West Pan Field, (the site of the Scottish

Camp, in 1644), and had a toll house and turnpike gate which stood near the site now occupied by the railway station. This gate was kept for some years, about the middle of the 18th century, by a man named Robin, who acquired the title " Robin o' the Yett," a name which continued to be applied to that part of the road, long after the removal of the toll gate. An annual hopping, or rural fair, and sports were held on this road, after the enclosure of Bishopwearmouth Green, 1799.

The sports included ass races, foot races, and climbing the greasy pole.

Wearmouth Walk THE portion of High Street from Bridge Street to Sunderland Street, was called Wearmouth Walk. On the north side there were successive rows of substantially built three storey houses occupied by well known shipowners, doctors, and tradesmen.

Each house had a neat flower garden and a pear tree covering the front of the house. The gardens were protected by an iron palisading and the footpath in front, for many years a favourite promenade for the inhabitants of Bishopwearmouth, was paved with small round stone from the beach.

Opposite to the Walk, on the south side of High Street, was the mansion known as Sunniside, occupied by Jacob Maude, Esq. There were extensive grounds attached to this house and an orchard which extended to Borough Road, then a country lane leading to Manor Farm. When High Street became the chief business centre of the town, shops were erected on the garden plots in front of the houses on the walk.

Sunniside was pulled down about the same time, and stately shops built where the mansion had stood. Many years afterwards, as the town grew and increased these shops were in turn levelled to the ground and Backhouse's Bank erected on the site of what was then the best business position in Sunderland.

East of Wearmouth Walk, the High Street continued as an open country road until Sunderland was reached and there too, more than two hundred years ago, were fine mansions or sea-side residences, with their pleasant gardens, occupied by the Lambtons, Tempests, Pembertons, and Lilburns.

These old mansions, which had formerly panelled rooms and carved oak staircases, are each now occupied by several tenants and have completely lost their former grandeur.

Hendon and Hendon Dene No part of Sunderland has changed as much, or grown so rapidly, as the district of Hendon. Less than one hundred years ago, the whole neighbourhood was covered by pleasant meadows, corn fields, market gardens, plantations, and a few farms and mansions.

The well known business centre called Hendon Road, was then a beautiful country lane known as Hendon Lonnin' and had tall trees and hawthorn hedges on each side. The lane commenced near Nicholson Square (now Nicholson Street), and near the first field, commonly called Coxon's field, stood the toll house and turnpike gate named Dickey's gate, after the toll keeper. Walking southward along this pleasant lane the pedestrian would pass Bowmaker's mill, a stone building dating from 1756; a large brick garth, or brick field; Burlinson's ropery; private gardens and orchards; Butterfint's Mill, a brick erection, built in 1822; the field in which the Archery Club met; the White House; the Cottage

Tavern; and finally would reach Noble's gardens near the entrance of which was a long two storied building used as a granary and storage place for hay and straw. Over the entrance was a board with the warning :—

"Man traps and spring guns in this garden."

Smaller rustic lanes branched from Hendon Lonnin', one led to Building Hill, others led to Hendon Lodge, Hendon House, and Field House. Each of these mansions was surrounded by gardens and plantations. The Lane leading to Hendon House, extended to the mouth of Hendon burn where the Bath house stood and where visitors could have hot or cold sea-water baths. This bathing establishment overlooked the pleasant Hendon Bay, where collier brigs were often seen waiting the tide before proceeding to the Wear.

"Fower Colliers lay in Hendon Bay
At anchor for the tide,
The 'Saucy Jane,' and the 'Eden Main,'
The 'Fox,' and the 'Rover's Bride.'"

Hendon Old Mill A WELL known object in the district was the ancient wooden stob-mill, one of the oldest of our sixteen local wind mills of the past. It stood on a huge post which was marked all over with names and dates; some of the latter far back into the 18th century, the earliest one being 1716. The mill was turned round to the wind by pushing a long beam which projected from behind. May Butterfint occupied this mill and the adjoining house for many years and during one of the terrible easterly gales on the coast, the mill was blown over. By the ingenuity of Sunderland ship-yard workmen it was soon replaced in its old position by means of strong shears and tackle, under the direction of Ben Dodds and his gang of riggers. The old mill was accidentally destroyed by fire and a new one raised on the same spot. At a later date this second wooden mill was pulled down and a large stone mill erected in its place.

Nothing now remains of the Hendon mills, but the street named Old Mill Road marks the place where they stood.

The building of residential property began at Hendon in 1835, when Doctor Ward erected a row of houses in Hendon Lonnin' and named the row Ward Terrace. Each house had an extensive garden in front and the whole terrace was enclosed by a brick wall and had large iron gates at the entrance. Sunderland folks called the terrace, " Ward's Folly," for, said they, in the local dialect "whe was gawn to live in such an out-of-the-world place as that ?"

In 1840 Cumberland Terrace was built overlooking the Hendon valley, and the grounds attached to the houses extended to the stream at the bottom. These dwellings, occupied by shipowners and merchants, had a splendid sea view and immediately opposite was an extensive meadow in which stood the last windmill erected at Hendon.

After this the rural aspect of Hendon diminished year by year. Three large rope walks were established in the neighbourhood and fields and gardens gave place to houses. The mansions already mentioned have been succeeded by streets of houses. Whitehouse Road marks the site of the White House and grounds. Hendon House is now the International Hotel, and on the carriage drive and gardens have arisen Henry, Addison, and Bramwell Streets, named after one of the proprietors of the mansion. Field House, once an important private school, with its extensive grounds has given place to Hudson Road, and numerous streets in the vicinity.

Hendon Dene The coast of Durham is remarkable for its many charming miniature valleys called "Denes." In former days they were beautifully wooded and noted for their rare ferns and flowers and as the homes of many birds and butterflies. The working of coal mines in the vicinity of the coast has deprived these little valleys of much of their former beauty and interest, but Castle Eden Dene, Hesledon Dene, Hawthorn Dene, Seaham Dene, and Ryhope Dene still provide some profit for the student of natural history. Castle Eden Dene is the largest and most beautiful. It contains no traces of the castle, which during the Norman times was occupied by Robert the Bruce, an ancestor of King Robert Bruce of Scotland.

The botonist may still find here the much prized British orchid the "lady's slipper" and also many valuable ferns and mosses. It is likewise the habitat of a very rare butterfly which is found nowhere else in the North of England.

At Sunderland we have Roker Ravine, one of the smaller denes, which adds much to the beauty of Roker Park. Lowther Dene and Robinson's Dene were once favourite resorts connected with the ancient Town Moor, but they have long ago disappeared. Many natives of Sunderland can describe Hendon Dene and Hendon valley. It was a place of exquisite beauty with its magnificent beech trees, its grassy slopes covered with flowers, and the rustic bridge across the sparkling brook which flowed through the valley to the sea. The valley extended from Ryhope Road to the sea. The eastern portion of the valley was laid out as a place of public recreation and pleasure, and called Hendon Valley Gardens. The attractions included foot races, walking contests, baloon ascents, and perhaps the most famous of all, an exhibition by Blondin who walked on a rope stretched across the valley, high above the heads of the people.

There were also public gardens in Ryhope Road (Victoria Gardens), and Tunstall Road (Strawberry Garden). These with the Hendon Dene, or Hendon Valley, or Valleys of Love, (we give all the names by which it was known) and the Hendon Valley Gardens provided pleasant places of recreation and social enjoyment to a generation which as yet, had no public parks.

There are many legends and stories connected with Hendon Dene, but space will only admit of the following :—

Nearly one hundred years ago, during a severe north east gale, a vessel was noticed drifting towards Hendon beach. People ran along the coast towards the spot where the ship was likely to strand. On reaching Hendon Burn they found that the water covered the stepping stones and they were unable to get across. Some of the men pushed a bathing machine into the burn to bridge it over, but the flood swept it into the sea. They therefore had to go round by Noble's Gardens, and on reaching Hendon banks it was seen that the ship had run " bow on " right into the dene and was in perfect safety. The crew were found stowing the sails, and the Captain was leaning over the bulwarks quietly smoking his pipe, with a grassy bank within six feet of him. The ship was got off at the spring tide, three weeks later.

H

CHAPTER VII.

THE HANOVERIAN PERIOD, PART 2.

Sunderland in the time of George III — During this period, Sunderland was composed of five different Townships or Parishes, viz: Bishopwearmouth, Bishopwearmouth Panns, and Sunderland on the South of the Wear, and Monkwearmouth and Monkwearmouth Shore on the north. Each parish had its own Overseers and was separately rated for the poor. It was a prosperous town with a population of about 30,000 inhabitants. The three principal streets were High Street, Low Street, and Coronation Street. High Street, which then consisted chiefly of residential property, extended from Low Row in Bishopwearmouth to the Fishermen's Cottages at the east end of Sunderland, where two flights of stone steps led down to the pier; whilst the road turning sharply to the right made its way to the beach. Low Street, then the principal manufacturing district of the town, extended from the Bridge to the mouth of the river. The narrow steep streets between High Street and Low Street were known as lanes, stairs, passages and banks. Coronation Street, or the Back Lonnin', was almost parallel to the High Street, and extended from Sunderland Parish Church to the back of Norfolk Street. The Streets communicating between High Street and Coronation Street were called lanes, alleys, and streets. South Street, as the name denotes, was the most southerly street in Bishopwearmouth, and Middle Street stood between High Street and South Street. On the west side of Crowtree Road was a high stone wall which

Iron Bridge, Wearmouth. 1796.
from an Old Engraving

was continued up Vine Place to the oldest house in Bishopwearmouth. This was a fine stone-built mansion, with gardens and vineries enclosed by the wall already mentioned and which also formed a protection for the high trees where the rooks built their nests.

West of Crowtree Road were Fenwick Lodge and Nicholson House. The former is still standing, but on the site of the latter Green Terrace Council School was erected in 1909. Other streets in this locality were:—Green Terrace, Low Row, Church Lane, South Gate, and Little Gate.

The portion of High Street belonging to Bishopwearmouth has already been described in Chapter VI. On the south side of High Street, between Sans Street (where Sunderland commenced) and George Street, the ground was much higher than the street level and was supported by a strong stone wall. This high ground formed a natural terrace, on which stood a number of well-built houses with fine tall trees in front, called the "High Justice Trees." From Maud's Lane to Grey Street there was a second terrace with trees known as the "Low Justice Trees." When this raised ground was lowered, the cellars of the houses were then on a level with the footpath, and were converted into shops which were for many years the principal places of business in old Sunderland. The houses on the east side of Lambton Street looked upon green fields which extended to Bridge Street; and the only residences then in Bridge Street were one on each side of the road near the bridge, and one on each side, at the High Street end of Bridge Street. The two latter had extensive gardens and vineries; one was the residence of Mr. Clanny.

The Market THE weekly market was held in High Street, most of the business being done on the north side of the street. The centre of the market place was once marked by a stone cross, which is supposed to have been destroyed during the Civil Wars. From this place were announced the rates at which wages had been fixed; descriptions of evil-doers wanted by the Justices; and such like proclamations. It was also the favourite place for hiring servants. The seed and corn market was held in front of the Exchange, and in close proximity was the Pig Market. The Poultry, Butter, and Egg Market was near Queen Street, and the butchers' stalls were situated between Water Lane and Beehive Lane; then came the stalls for boots and shoes; fruit and potatoes; crabs, lobsters, oysters, etc.

The Fish Market was held on the Quay in Low Street. The Fairs, held in May and October, occupied the whole of High Street from Sans Street to the end of the town; the shows and caravans were located in Barrack Street.

The tradesmen and manufacturers of the town at this period generally resided in the rooms above their shops or business premises.

Low Street contained Chain and Anchor Works, at the foot of Russell Street, and the busy workshops and yards occupied by coopers, block and mast makers, smiths, nail makers, boat builders, sailmakers, and timber merchants. There were also three breweries and numerous quays for loading and discharging cargoes and ballast.

In the year 1820, there were 41 public houses in Low Street; in 1888 there were only 12, and in 1916 the number was reduced to 3. In former days these houses provided refreshments for sailors, keelmen, casters, labourers, corn porters, glassmen and carpenters.

The Unitarians had their place of meeting in Maling's Rigg; the Jews had a synagogue in Vine Street, the Calvinists had a Chapel down an entry near the old Corn Market; while the Roman Catholic Chapel was in Dunning Street. A few of the oldest lanes and alleys have been pulled down and model dwellings erected in James Williams Street and on the site of the Hat Case.

The streets were lighted by oil lamps fastened to the wall or the corner of the houses at the end of the street or lane. Each lamp had to be trimmed every morning, and supplied with sufficient oil to keep it burning from lighting up time until daylight next morning. The houses were chiefly illuminated by common tallow candles, made in the town, mould candles, or rushlights; the shops and stalls in the Market Place were lighted by oil lamps with cotton wicks.

There were no lucifer matches in those days; every housewife had to have a tinder box, flint, and steel in order to light the fire, etc. The streets were patrolled at night by watchmen, each carrying a staff and a lantern. They were generally elderly men nick-named "old Charlies." Watch boxes were erected in which they could shelter on wet nights, but they had to make their rounds every half hour and call out the time and the state of the weather, thus:—

"Twelve o'clock, and a starlight night!"
"Past one o'clock, fine morning, all's well!"

Water Supply   WATER for household purposes was obtained from the numerous springs, wells and pumps. There were twenty pumps in Sunderland Parish alone. The ships frequenting the port were supplied from the pumps in Water Lane and Bodlewell Lane, and from the Castle Well at Lambton coal staithes.

There were several pumps in Bishopwearmouth Parish, two were in the Rectory Grounds, one on the Green, and one at the foot of Durham Road, where the present drinking fountain stands. The following announcement illustrates the manner in which many of the inhabitants of Bishopwearmouth were supplied with water :—

"LOW SPRING WATER AT THE IMPROVED PATENT ROPERY IN BISHOPWEARMOUTH.

The inhabitants of Bishopwearmouth are respectfully informed that they may now be supplied with excellent water at the improved patent ropery in South Street, at a farthing a skeel on the spot, and by water-cart at a halfpenny a skeel at their own homes. N.B. This water is found to make excellent tea water, and answers well for washing."

The public water supply at Monkwearmouth was obtained from three wells, two of which were the property of Sir Hedworth Williamson, they were situated near the Parish Church and known respectively as the High Pump and the Low Pump ; but the best water was obtained from the Union Well, belonging to the proprietors of the Blue Factory Estate. The water from the Union Well was sent round Monkwearmouth in water-carts and sold at a half-farthing per skeel. On each cart were the following lines :—

"It's limpid, and clear from all mud,
This water I sell for the public good ;
Its excellent virtues no mortal can tell,
So sweet is the water from Union Well."

The usual charge for water was a bodle (half-farthing) per skeelful. The "skeel"— the word is derived from the Icelandic " skeola," meaning a milk pail,—was a wooden tub or bucket narrower at the top than at the base, and having one of its staves prolonged upwards to form a handle. These skeels were about as large as a woman could lift on to her head when full, and to carry them more comfortably, she would use a circular roll or twist of straw or wool, called a "weeze" placed on her head underneath the skeel.

It was noted that the women and girls of Sunderland acquired an upright and graceful walk due to carrying the skeels of water upon their heads.

Coaches and Sedan Chairs

THERE were three modes of travelling :—on foot, on horseback, and in carriages. Rich people travelled in their own carriages, or they hired carriages and paid one shilling a mile per horse. The Stage Coach was a public vehicle and professed to travel about seven miles an hour, the charge being three pence per mile. From the year 1784, the coaches also carried mails. The "Golden Lion" was the chief coaching inn for Sunderland; the "Peacock Inn" for Bishopwearmouth; and the "Old Oak Tree Inn" for Monkwearmouth.

The Stockton coach had four horses, and the Durham and Newcastle coaches had each three. By the former the traveller could book to Thirsk, Leeds, York, and London; but many Sunderland people journeying to London, preferred going first to Newcastle where several coaches set out for London. The fare from Sunderland to Newcastle was 2/6 outside and 5/- inside. In 1836, the Highflyer was advertised as making the journey from Newcastle to London in 36 hours.

The Guard of the Mail Coach wore a red coat and always had his long trumpet in its socket, except when blowing a blast as the coach was coming to a corner round which it had to turn. He was also provided with a blunderbuss for the protection of the mails and the passengers.

In addition to the Mail Coaches, sedan chairs were frequently to be seen in Sunderland streets in bygone times. The Sedan Chair was a high box with a door in front, in which a window was inserted ; and there was a seat inside for the occupier. Two long poles were attached to the chair and it was carried by two bearers one in front and one behind. Sometimes a third man was engaged to carry a link or torch to light them on their way. If the ladies of the town wished to attend a ball or a play, they usually went in Sedan Chairs. The last of the Sedan Chairs in Sunderland, was kept for hire by John Watkin who resided in High Street East. In 1818 it was frequently to be seen standing near the entrance of his house.

The proprietor, who was one of the parish constables, had been a petty officer in the Navy. He was a short, stout-built man, and wore a low crowned broad brimmed hat, blue coat, velveteen breeches, worsted stockings and had buckles on his shoes.

The Ballast Hills THE wooden ships which traded to Sunderland during this period always arrived laden with ballast which was discharged either at the Ballast Quays in Low Street, or just below the ferry boat landing at Monkwearmouth. At the latter place the ballast was taken up through a tunnel which led from the Quay to the top of the bank. It was then taken in carts and deposited on the ground now occupied by Dame Dorothy Street, Dock Street, and other streets in the locality. In the course of time this changed the whole contour of the ground at Monkwearmouth from Church Street eastwards. The old Workhouse and its grounds, which occupied the site of Zetland Street, were covered with ballast ; in fact the Workhouse, after the windows, doors, etc., were taken away, was practically buried in the immense deposits of ballast. Tons of ballast were also deposited around the ancient church, so that it now stands in a hollow, instead on what was once comparatively high ground. The four hills of Monkwearmouth Shore were all formed by these deposits. Large ballast hills were also formed at Deptford and Southwick.

Illustrious Visitors   THERE were several important visitors to Sunderland in the reign of George III. Daniel Defoe, the author of Robinson Crusoe, visited our town in 1762 ; the Duke of Gloucester in 1796, Sir Henry Vane Tempest in 1812 ; and the Emperor of Russia in 1816. In Defoe's account of his visit to the North Country he states :—

"The air in the County of Durham is pretty cold and piercing, and 'tis well for the poor that Nature has supplied them so abundantly with fuel for firing. It seems as if the whole county had been originally appropriated to Religion and War, for it is full of ruins of religious houses and castles. The people of Sunderland were hard at work deepening their harbour and building a pier, and I was struck by the bustle and prosperity of the town ; by the fineness of its streets and its appearance of wealth and comfort."

CHAPTER VIII.

ANCIENT CUSTOMS, SPORTS, AND PUNISHMENTS.

Perambulating the Boundaries

THIS old custom is mentioned in Bishop Morton's Charter of 1154. It referred not only to the common lands, but also to the boundaries of the township. It was customary for the authorities to walk round the boundaries at certain periods, and to remove any obstacles or buildings that had been erected without permission.

Sunderland was made a separate parish in 1719, and the first perambulation of the Parish of Sunderland was made on the 3rd of September, 1811.

The perambulators, under a merry peal of the five old bells of the Parish Church, headed by the Rector and the Parish Officers, with their official wands, proceeded up Coronation Street, then called "The Back Lonnin'," at different parts of which, and upon the boundary line adjoining Bishopwearmouth, "S.P." for Sunderland Parish, was for the first time painted up, and a plentiful supply of gingerbread nuts thrown away among the youngsters. They then passed down Sans Street and Beggars' Bank (Russell Street), at the foot of which several cobles were in waiting (steam boats at that time being unknown). Here the party embarked and proceeded down the river to the sea, where they took a good offing to claim the boundaries of the parish down to low water mark. The perambulators landed from the cobles on the beach at the "way foot" in the Dene at the south end of the Town Moor, led on by Mr. Paxton, joiner, an aged man, who well knew that part of the

Hylton Castle in 1746.

southern boundary of the parish from his father, having been for many years the herd of the cattle stinted upon the Town Moor. They then passed up the middle of the small stream on the south side of the Octagon Cottage.

On entering the plantation of Hendon Lodge, now the site of Moor Terrace, etc., John Mailing, Esq., grandfather of the late C. M. Webster, of Pallion Hall, joined the perambulators, and assisted Mr. Paxton in pointing out the Sunderland part of the Bishop of Durham's Waste, upon which portion of the drawing room and kitchen of Hendon Lodge were built, and through these rooms some of the perambulators passed.

At a subsequent perambulation in 1845, in addition to the usual liberal distribution of gingerbread nuts, a large quantity of half-farthings, brought from London expressly for the occasion, were thrown amongst the youngsters.

One of the leaders in the perambulating of Bishopwearmouth Parish was the well known Dicky Chilton. He assisted the men who carried axes to demolish unwarranted wooden posts set up to prevent the people from using ancient public footpaths. On these occasions there was always a man with a paint pot to mark the exact limits of the parish ; another to scatter gingerbread nuts for the children, and a fiddler to enliven them with his music.

The inhabitants, headed by that ancient dignitary the Greeve of Wearmouth, also walked round the enclosed shrubbery, all that remained of the ancient Village Green.

Thus the Greeve of Wearmouth and the inhabitants exercised a legal right upon this the only remaining part of the wastes within the greeveship which had belonged equally to the lord and the parishoners for nearly 180 years after the diverson and enclosure of the moors, commons, and wastes, in Bishopwearmouth, during the Commonwealth.

The last of the perambulations of the boundaries of the common land known as the Burn Fields, was in the year 1824.

Saint Crispin's Day   ONE hundred years ago the shoemakers of Sunderland were known by the name of cordwainers. They supplied the inhabitants of the town with hand made boots, shoes, and wooden clogs. Local tanneries suppied the leather which was dressed in curriers' shops in the town. Sunderland at this time was noted for its excellent boots and shoes which were exported to Norway, Sweden, and to the American Colonies ; 277 pairs being sent to the Colonies in 1818.

The cordwainers held their annual procession on the 25th of October in honour of Saint Crispin, their patron saint.

The procession, headed by a band of music, started from the Town Moor. In the front ranks were the master cordwainers. ; following these the journeymen and apprentices ; and bringing up the rear, individuals employed by the masters, who did their work in their respective homes. From time to time as the procession paraded the principal streets of our town, its ranks were joined by tanners and curriers, all enthusiastic followers of Saint Crispin.

Cloy Day in Sunderland   ANOTHER ancient custom was the celebration of Saint Cloy, the patron saint of the smiths, which was held by Sunderland smiths on the 21st of June, locally known as Cloy Day.

The Smiths' Miracle Play and the celebration of Cloy Day are supposed to have been introduced by Sir Ambrose Crowley's workmen in 1682. The day was not set apart as a holiday, but the master smith, who at that period worked with his men, provided them with a substantial dinner. To begin Cloy Day the men, of their own free will, agreed to be at the shop by five o'clock in the morning. They worked until twelve o'clock when they were called to dinner after which one of the senior workmen told the following story of the origin of the feast :—

"There was once a very rich gentleman named Cloy who built a large house or castle. When it was nearly finished he invited all the workmen to partake of his hospitality. By some mistake he forgot to invite the smiths, and so they agreed amongst themselves that they would not go to work again until the gentleman found out his mistake.

The day after the feast when the men were about to resume their work it was found that there was no smith to sharpen the tools and so the work was at a standstill. Then came the foreman smith and cried aloud :—

'With my hammer in hand,
All trades do stand.'

The clerk of the works informed the gentleman that they could do nothing at all, because the smiths had struck work. So he came and heard what the smiths had to say. Then he told them to go to work, and at the completion of the building he would give another dinner to which they should be invited.

When the day for the feast arrived the smiths occupied the place of honour, at the top of the table, as they not only made their own tools, but also the working tools required by every class of workmen."

The last Cloy Day was held on the 21st of June, 1817, by the ship and whitesmiths employed at Queen Street. Having several small cannon to fit up and mount on gun carriages for ships as stern chasers, they loaded one of the pieces, putting in a good charge of powder and using oakum and rope for wadding. Not having a ramrod, they took a bar of iron to ram the charge down, and to make sure of a good report (as a salute for Cloy Day), they took a sledge hammer to knock it in. The result was that the bar could not be withdrawn.

It was decided to fire the gun, with the bar of iron in it, straight up the middle of Queen Street.

As a necessary precaution, four lads were sent up to the top of the street, to the Back Lonnin', to let no one pass either up or down.

When all was clear the cannon was discharged and the bar of iron was sent over Zion Street into the country towards Ryhope, and was never found.

The result of this wonderful salute was that all the windows of the Phœnix Masonic Lodge were broken, as well as those in the large house opposite, the only houses then in the neighbourhood. The master smith had to repair the damaged property and pay all expenses, and there were no more celebrations of Cloy Day for his men after that. On the same day, when the smiths at Folly End, on the north side of the river, celebrated Cloy Day a sad accident occurred and one of the workmen lost his right hand. This was also the last Cloy Day for Monkwearmouth.

How Naval Victories were Announced The custom of people singing in the street early in the morning of Christmas Day is probably derived from an ancient Saxon custom known as yollwaytyng or yulewaiting. In Bishop Pudsey's time yulewaiting was a regular system of service due from certain tenants to the Lord of the Manor and probably it had reference to service with which must be connected the protection of that manor house in which the Bishop happened to be residing during the festivities of Christmas.

Closely connected with yulewaiting we have the "Waits" or watchmen. In ancient times they were minstrels, at first attached to the King's court, who sounded the watch every night, and paraded the streets for the protection of the people.

The minstrelsy of the Waits was continued in Sunderland for centuries, down to the year 1809, when the first Sunderland Improvement Act was passed, and regular watchmen appointed.

The last of the Waits who traversed the streets and lanes of Sunderland and serenaded the inhabitants with nocturnal music was George Stephenson. He played his fiddle at regular places, after which Jacob Wade, his partner cried out "Good morrow masters and dames all," then gave the hour and the direction from which the wind blew.

The Waits were also engaged to make announcements to the people of the victories gained by British valour during the wars of the French Revolution. At that time a few men who resided at Sunderland openly avowed themselves admirers of the Jacobins of France.

The naval victories of :—
The Glorious 1st of June, 1794.
St. Vincent, 14th February 1797.
Camperdown, 11th October, 1797.
The Nile, 1st August, 1798, and
Trafalgar, 21st October, 1805,
were all announced in our ancient town by the Waits accompanied by crowds of loyal inhabitants who invariably paid a visit to the sympathisers of France, before whose doors Stephenson played a patriotic air, followed by Wade proclaiming the victory, and the crowd giving such hearty British cheers as struck terror to the Jacobin enemies of their country.

Cock Fighting at Sunderland
THIS was a recognised sport in the days when people had fewer intellectual pastimes or pleasures than they have now.
The spread of education, science, art, and literature have produced a beneficial change in the habits, customs, and tastes of the public, and none will regret that the brutalising sports of cock-fighting and bull-baiting are things of the past.

Squire Stafford, of Monkwearmouth, was celebrated as a great breeder of game cocks, and on one occasion he won the County Prize for the best bird. The prize consisted of a full sized game cock, cast in gold, and it is said that he was so delighted with the prize that he placed it on top of one the columns of the " Babbies " which stood at the entrance of his house in Broad Street (now called Roker Avenue) so that his neighbours and fellow townsmen might admire it.

Squire Stafford's residence was one of the oldest mansions in Monkwearmouth. It had been originally built by a member of the Abbs' family and stood at the corner of Fulwell Lane and Broad Street, on the site now occupied by Mr. Craven's Ropery.

The mansion had a massive clock at the top of the building which struck the hours in loud and sonorous tones.

The twelve leaden statues of life-size figures brought from Holland, and known as the "Babbies" were fixed on the walls from Portobello Lane down Fulwell Road, to where now stands the Church of All Saints. Two of these figures, representing Spring and Summer, can now be seen in Roker Park.

A row of lofty lime trees, forming a home for numerous rooks extended round the estate. The last of these fine trees was blown down during a gale on the 23rd of November, 1857.

Cock-fighting led to breeding, rearing, and training game fowl, and a game cock who slew his opponents was the pride of a whole town or countryside. Vast sums of money were won or lost over the combats of these birds.

When a cock was matched to fight he was put into the care of a trainer to prepare him for the battle. His feathers and comb were trimmed and his natural spurs reduced to about half an inch in length, to allow for steel spurs, each about two and a half inches long and with a socket at one end, being fixed on the natural spur of each leg. These artificial spurs were thin and very sharp at the point.

The combat usually took place in a properly prepared cock pit or cock ring which was sunk in the ground and around this inner circle was an outer one raised a few feet for the benefit of the spectators.

Each cock had a second, or handler, as he was called, whose duty it was to take it into the pit and see that the rules agreed upon were properly carried out.

At the end of each " round " the cocks were separated for a short interval of rest. These fights were often very exciting and every advantage one bird gained over his antagonist brought forth rounds of cheers from his backers. The pluck and endurance of game cocks when fighting is marvellous ; they fight to the death and only yield with their last breath.

Some of our ancient street names indicate where the combats took place. We have Fighting Cock Tavern, Fighting Cock Yard, Black Cock Inn, Black Cock Open, and Fighting Cock Lane in our town, and there were also private cock pits in the district ; one was on Wreath Hills and the remains of another may still be seen in a field to the west of Barnes Park. There was also a cock-pit in Low Row, behind some old cottages near the burn, where it is said, the last cock-fight took place in Bishopwearmouth.

Bull Baiting at Sunderland The bull-ring was formerly a national institution and in every large town there was an open space used for the purpose of bull-baiting. The last bull-bait on Bishopwearmouth Green was held in the year 1788. In the centre of the Green was a large stone with an iron ring fixed in it, to which the ropes attached to the bull were fastened. The poor animal could thus only run round a circle, the length of the rope being the radius, whilst savage bull-dogs attacked him.

In old Sunderland the cruel sport took place on the Town Moor, the last bull-bait being held on the 29th of May, 1822.

The bull was provided by one of the butchers and the rope to which it was attached was fastened to an anchor firmly fixed in the ground. The circle in which the bull was baited was staked round with ropes and no persons were admitted inside the circle except the owners of the dogs.

These dogs had been carefully trained to fly at the bull, seize him by the nose or ear, and hold on until the bull threw them off. Sometimes a dog was caught on the bull's horns and tossed into the air.

After the sport had continued for some time the bull generally became fagged and would not run. The dogs were then called off and the bull was led away to the slaughter house.

Not only was bull-baiting looked upon with favour as a means of sport, but was considered useful in another way as the flesh of the bull was thought to be improved by baiting the animal.

Fox Hunting at Sunderland
Fox hunting has always been regarded as the favourite sport of country gentlemen and when Bishopwearmouth and Sunderland were little country towns the gentlemen residing in the district established what was known as the "Bishopwearmouth Independent Hunt."* During the fox hunting season the members met once or twice a week near the corner of Stockton Road, a little to the west of the premises now occupied by Mr. R. Crow, Auctioneer.

This was a convenient place for meeting as five country lanes met at this point. The place is entirely changed in appearance now. It was then an open grass-

* The Sunderland Hunt, established in 1811, was supported by annual subscriptions of ten guineas.

covered space bordered by tall trees and hedges and having an old pump and water trough in the centre. There were only two houses in the immediate vicinity, the old farm, now in the occupation of Messrs Borrowdale Brothers, the Sculptors and Granite Workers, and the oldest house in Bishopwearmouth, on the site of which stands the Technical College.

Here the huntsmen in their scarlet coats, the master of the hunt, and the hounds assembled.

Amongst the members would be found the gentry residing at Vine Lodge, The Grange, Cresswell House, Eden House, Hunter's Hall, Thornhill, Bainbridge Holme, West Lodge, High Barnes and Low Barnes, Farringdon Hall, Herrington Hall, Grindon House, Fenwick Lodge, Nicholson House, Biddick Hall, Lambton Hall, Ford Hall, Pallion Hall, Frederick Lodge, and Deptford Hall.

Members of Monkwearmouth district came from Monkwearmouth Hall, Monkwearmouth Grange, Whitburn Hall, Cleadon Towers, Washington Hall, Usworth Hall and other residences.

Sir Hedworth Williamson, the sixth Bartonet, was a keen sportsman and doubtless a member of the hunt. He kept a pack of harriers and on two occasions won the Derby in 1803 with a horse called "Ditto," and in 1808 with another named "Pan."

It is said that Squire Stafford and the "Hunting Parson" seldom missed a meeting of the hounds.

We have only space to give particulars of a remarkable run after Reynard which took place on the 20th of February, 1770. The chase commenced at Newbottle, where a fox was turned out of the wood closely followed by the hounds. A hare started across the fox's track, but poor puss was quickly run to earth. After this little diversion, they again got scent of the fox and had a smart run for twelve miles, when the fox eluded them by leaping down a lime-kiln and creeping out at the "eye." The hounds were again got on the track, but soon afterwards lost scent for some time by the fox running through a conduit, after which he leaped down a rock and swam across the river. Not being pursued he ventured to return, but here he was again scented and the hounds were soon after him in full cry. After giving his pursuers another long run of nearly fourteen miles, Reynard just saved his brush by leaping on board a ship in the river at Ayre's Quay, where he was captured alive by the sailors.

Horse Racing on the Moor

DURING the early part of the eighteenth century, horse racing was frequently held on the Town Moor and large numbers of people assembled to witness the sport.

One of the last occasions was on the 19th and 20th of September, 1732, when prizes to the total value of £110 were awarded to the owners of the winning horses. The races were afterwards held at Tunstall Hope.

Bowling on the Moor

THIS was a favourite sport in ancient times when nearly every Inn had its bowling green. The bowling course on the Moor ran from north to south. In playing the game, at Sunderland, each bowler had an assistant called a tracker, who walked before the bowler and pointed out the best or most convenient spot for the bowl to beat on when thrown.

Wherever the bowler picked up his bowl his jacket was laid, and from that spot he must give the next throw, and so on to the end of the course.

Bowlers in former days generally made their own bowls. They were made of blue stone, which they picked up off the beach and which had been washed out of the clay banks by the action of the waves. The stones thus found were chipped with little hammers and rubbed against harder stones until they were perfectly smooth and rounded to fit the hands of the owner. The bowls were of different sizes and weights, according to the skill of the players. The Sunderland keelmen were the most skilful players of bowls on the Moor.

Riding the Stang THE now obsolete practice of riding the stang was frequently carried out at Sunderland in ancient times; the unfortunate victims of this mob-law being those who had in some way or other rendered themselves objectionable to their neighbours.

The custom evidently originated in Saxon times, and the word stang or steng meant a pole, bar, or shaft. It is mentioned in Bishop Pudsey's Charter (Chapter V), that "stengesduit" ought not to exist in the Borough.

Canon Greenwell translates the Saxon word "stengesduit" as meaning a fine inflicted for an assault committed with a stick or like instrument (steng, a club or pole, and duit, a fine).

The practice of riding the stang was well known in the north of England and Scotland and it was not unlike the custom known in the south of England under the name "To ride Skimmington."

The stang consisted of a plank or pole, carried upon the shoulders of men or lads, and on which the unlucky culprit was mounted. He was thus paraded through the streets of the town, exposed to the assults and ridicule of the crowd who followed him, the proceedings being enlivened by the music of old tin pans, kettles, horns, and other like melodious instruments.

One of the most remarkable instances of stang-riding occurred at the close of the first American War, when the sailors of Sunderland got liberty to go on shore, having been kept on board their ships during the war for fear of being kidnapped by the press-gang.

On the 13th of February, 1783, great numbers of sailors assembled and proceeded to the houses of those who had acted as informers to the press-gang. All they could lay hands on were compelled to submit to the ignominious ordeal of riding the stang, and the constables who interfered to protect them from the fury of the mob were completely overpowered and beaten off. Towards evening things had assumed so serious an aspect that the North York Militia Regiment, then quartered in the town, had to turn out to disperse the mob. Amongst the victims of these lawless proceedings was Jonathan Coates, commonly called "Jotty Coates," then living in Arras's Lane, who was so roughly dealt with "on the stang" that on being liberated he was more dead than alive. However, he managed to crawl home, but, hearing a noise in the street during the night, and thinking his tormentors were coming in search of him again, he crawled into a narrow gully in the neighbourhood, where his lifeless body was found the following morning.

About ten years after this occurrence the last case of riding the stang is recorded in Sunderland.

This arose out of the keelsmen's strike, when Nicholas Lowes, a keelman, was accused of informing against those who blockaded the river by mooring their keels in the channel, and entangling the anchors and cables. Nicholas was paraded through the town on a stang, but seven of the men who took a prominent part in the affair were tried at the ensuing Durham Assizes, and sentenced to two years imprisonment.

This ancient custom throws some light on the cruel and lawless methods by which public opinion expressed its resentment more than 120 years ago.

We may rejoice that we live in an age when the mob can no longer take the law into its own hands.

The Cage, Stocks, and Pillary THE place for detention of prisoners awaiting trail was a small cell with a grated window, called the Cage. At Sunderland the cell was situated near the Church, at the east end of Coronation Street, and in the district was known as the "Kitty." It still remains but is now used for another purpose. At Monkwearmouth the Cage was erected on the top of Cage Hill, at Monkwearmouth Shore. This cell was of small dimensions, but had huge stone walls, an iron door, and barred windows.

For such offences as drunkenness, brawling, and petty theft, the magistrates often sentenced the offender to two, three, or four hours in the Stocks, according to the gravity of the offence. In Stuart times "sturdy beggars," that is, those strong enough to work, were by order of the Justice of Peace, placed in the stocks for a considerable period and were then compelled to leave the village.

Confinement in the Stocks was an ancient method of punishment. A law was passed by King Edward III in 1376, commanding that Stocks should be set up in every town and village, and in some parts of England they were in use until 1865. The Stocks consisted of a wooden bench or seat, having a thick board in front of it with holes, in which the feet of the culprit were fixed. The delinquent was thus exposed to the gaze of people passing, and to the jeers of the men, women, and children who gathered in crowds to see those who were undergoing punishment.

It is said that the mode of punishment was so degrading that a drunkard seldom appeared more than once in that position.

The Stocks at Sunderland were kept in the Church porch and when in use were set up in the Market Place, near the foot of Church Street. Bishopwearmouth Stocks were fixed in the ground on the Village Green.

At Monkwearmouth the ancient Stocks were firmly fixed in the ground near the spot where the National School now stands. There is a local record connected with these Stocks and it appears that on the 15th of June, 1815, they were repaired at a cost of nine and sixpence and new keys were provided for the Cage at the same time for two shillings and sixpence.

The Pillory was a board with three holes in it, through which the offender's head and hands were thrust. In this position he was unable to move and was subjected to the jeers of the public who often pelted him with rotten eggs, decayed fruit, and other refuse. A baker who sold loaves which were short in weight, would be placed in the Pillory with one of his loaves hung round his neck and a fishmonger found guilty of selling bad fish would have a portion of the fish round his neck as he stood in the Pillory.

There is only one local reference to the use of the Pillory in Sunderland. This occurred on the 3rd of October, 1811, when a man named Thomas Elliott, stood in the Pillory for two hours, according to his sentence passed at the Assizes at Durham. The Pillory was erected upon a wooden platform about eight feet high, near the Market Cross, in High Street.

This mode of punishment was abolished by Act of Parliament in 1837.

CHAPTER IX.

The River Wear

FAR away to the west, among the dark mountains of the Pennines, rises the river to which Sunderland owes much of its importance ; a stream of no great length, yet holding its own among English rivers for the beauty of its scenery and the romantic character of its associations.

The Wear is formed by the junction of the Burnhope and Kilhope Burns, which unite at Wearhead Village, 1100 feet above the sea level. WEARHEAD is noted for the Burtree Pasture Lead Mine which contains the richest vein of lead in England. There are several Whinstone Quarries in the district and many beautiful trees, the most famous being the ancient Sycamore Trees near Cowshill.

About two miles from the source is IRESHOPE Village where a stream of the same name joins the Wear. Flowing through mountain scenery and frequent woods and plantations the river passes the Village of ST. JOHN'S where there are lead mines and a church dedicated to St. John the Baptist.

The course of the Wear through the dale is rapid ; the name being taken from a Celtic word which signifies "Rapid Water," but nearly all the small tributaries, called burns, retain the names given to them in Saxon times. The streams uniting with the Wear in its upper course flow from the high, bleak, and treeless moorlands,

*The Grange, Bishopwearmouth.
1789.*

which display great tracts of purple heather or yellow gorse in the autumn.

Below St. John's are two villages, about four miles apart, called WESTGATE and EASTGATE. These were formerly the West and East forest gates of the Prince Bishop's great hunting park. Near Westgate, where the Swinhope Burn joins the river, was once situated the Bishop's Hunting Castle of which nothing now remains. Eastgate was formerly the residence of the Bishop's Bailiff and here the Rookhope Burn joins the river Wear.

Roman Coins and a Roman Altar have been found in the woods near Eastgate.

STANHOPE, standing 670 feet above sea level and a few miles below Eastgate, is an ancient town and the capital of Weardale. There are many places of interest in and around this small country town. The present Stanhope Castle, erected in 1798, by Cuthbert Rippon, Esq., at one time a Member of Parliament for Gateshead, embowered in lofty trees occupies the site of an old fortified mansion existing in the time of Bishop Anthony Beck.

The fine old Norman Church built about the year 1200 ; the large market place with a stone cross and many beautiful lime trees, together with several ancient buildings and pre-historic and Roman remains found in the locality, are all worthy of a visit.

The visitor to Stanhope will also see several of the rarer British Birds including the Merlin, or Stone Falcon, Sparrow Hawk, Spotted Fly Catcher, Water Ousel, Golden Crested Wren, Blue Tit, Jay, Swift, Nightjar, Woodpecker, Snipe, the vividly coloured Kingfisher, and many rare and beautiful ferns and flowers. The stream joining the Wear at this place is known as the Stanhope Burn. The fine climate, beautiful woods, pleasant walks and so many interesting places to be seen, have all combined to make this little town famous as a holiday resort.

FROSTERLY is about two and a half miles below Stanhope. The name means Foresters' Lea, and indicates that it was one of the leys or open forest groves. It is famous for its large quarries which give employment to four hundred men. The well known Frosterly Marble comes from this district.

WOLSINGHAM, sixteen miles west of Durham, was originally one of the Bishop's Forest Vills. It contains many interesting old houses, and a Grammar School founded in 1612.

Past Wolsingham the Wear reaches WITTON-LE-WEAR, round which is found the most delightful river scenery. At this point is the junction of the lead measures with the coal fields.

Near this village is Witton Castle, erected in 1410, by Sir Ralph Eure. The building has been considerably altered at various periods. On the south east turret are two figures in armour.

At BISHOP AUCKLAND the river flows towards the north and here it receives the waters of the river Gaunless. In close proximity to the town is Bishop Auckland Castle the modern residence of the Bishops of Durham. It occupies a commanding position in a park of considerable size. The Castle was almost completely rebuilt by Bishop Cosin in 1666. One of its most prominent and interesting features is the Chapel, a fine structure in which several Bishops are buried.

Near Bishop Auckland is Binchester, where the remains of a Roman Camp are still to be seen.

Before reaching Durham the river passes Brancepeth Castle, near a village of the same name. The castle was built by Ralph, first Earl of Westmoreland, on the site of a former castle erected before the Norman Conquest by the family of Bulmer. The Baron's Hall is a beautiful room ornamented with stained glass windows, the west window representing views of the memorable Battle of Neville's Cross. It was in this hall that the northern gentry and their retainers met for the "Rising of the North," which brought about the outlawry of Neville, the owner of the Castle.

A small stream called the Hockley, runs through the Castle grounds and unites with the Wear. The ancient Church of St. Brandon, near the castle, contains several sepulchral effigies to members of the Neville family.

The City of DURHAM owes its fame and importance to its magnificent Cathedral and old Norman Castle. They stand side by side on the crest of a hill almost surrounded by the Wear, and together make Durham one of the most picturesque cities in the British Isles.

Durham Castle, built in 1072, contains many objects of great interest and the walls of Tunstall's Gallery are covered with 16th century tapestry.

The hall is 101 feet long, 35 feet wide and contains a celebrated collection of paintings, including portraits of Charles I, and Charles II ; thirteen portraits of Archbishops and Bishops and ten pictures of the Apostles.

It would require a large volume to do justice to the glories of the magnificent Cathedral of Durham. It has been called " A great poem in stone " and to fully appreciate the beauties of the Norman Nave, the Galilee, and the Chapel of the Nine Altars, it must be visited again and again.

Near Durham the Wear receives the Browney, its largest tributary. From Durham it flows, still beautiful, through the Cocken Woods, full of wild daffodils in the spring time.

The ruins of Finchale Priory are most romantically situated in a wooded valley, north of Durham.

> Where Vedra* gently flows through woodlands green,
> Midst crags and oaks the Priory may be seen,
> Rearing its ivy'd walls high o'er the trees
> In solemn grandeur.

Below Durham the river winds in a slower, calmer current towards that other place of ancient memories, MONKWEARMOUTH, whose Church is even older than the Cathedral itself.

CHESTER-LE-STREET, as its name implies, was once a Roman Station. During Saxon times, for nearly 120 years, it was the Christian Metropolis of the North. The early Cathedral Church was built of wood and here the Monks of Lindisfarne brought the body of St. Cuthbert when they fled before the Danes.

The present Church dates from the 13th century and is remarkable for the fourteen monumental effigies of presumed members of the Lumley family.

Lumley Castle, near Chester-le-Street, stands on an eminence overlooking the river, and having Lumley Burn on the North side. It was built by Sir Ralph Lumley in the reign of Edward I. The Castle hall is of considerable size and has a gallery for minstrels at the west end, and a striking series of portraits of the Lumleys.

* Roman name for the Wear.

Lambton Castle, eight miles from the mouth of the Wear, stands on the site of Harraton Hall, a mansion house erected in 1600. The south front of the Castle is built in the Tudor Style and is castellated, while the north front represents the Norman style of architecture. In the picture gallery are works of the famous artists Reynolds, Romney, Lawrence, Gainsborough, and Holbein. The great hall is panelled in oak and the stained glass windows contain a representation of :—
" Ye Legend of the Worme of Lambton."

This Castle is the principal seat of the third Earl of Durham, to the memory of whose grandfather Penshaw Monument was erected in the year 1844.

Hylton Castle, a few miles east of Lambton Castle, is on the north bank of the Wear on a gentle slope commanding an extensive view to the west. The first Castle was built on this site in 1072, but the present building is only the large Gate House of the Castle erected about the year 1260.

Over the entrance is a fine array of heraldry showing the arms of the well known families of Neville, Vesci, Percy, Lumley, Grey, Eure, Washington, Felton, Heron, Surtees, Bowes, and Hylton.

The river Wear, if followed from its source to the port of Sunderland, makes a panorama unrivalled in its way for picturesqueness. The mountain scenery of upper Weardale ; the numerious woods ; the eight noble Castles ; the glorious old Cathedral ; the monastic ruins of Finchale and the ancient Churches of Stanhope, Brancepeth, Chester-le-Street, Bishopwearmouth, and Monkwearmouth, will long be pleasant memories to the pedestrian who has followed the windings of the river.

CHAPTER X.

SHIPBUILDING.

Early History   THE art of constructing ships dates from remote antiquity, and we find in history many particulars of the ships in use in ancient times. In our local museum can be seen a pre-historic dug-out canoe, found in the bed of the river Wear near Hylton in 1885. It has been hewn out of an oak tree trunk and is estimated to be more than 2,000 years old. This may be claimed to be Sunderland's earliest boat, and the forerunner of the many noble vessels which have for centuries been built on the Wear, and have made Sunderland's reputation as the largest Shipbuilding town in the world. There is no doubt that Romans, Saxons, and Danes, built their vessels on the Wear. Year after year brought its improvements, century after century its changes, until the art of shipbuilding in wood approached perfection, and the rude row Galley of our forefathers gave place to the beautiful Clipper Ship, with its fine lines, tapering masts, and flowing canvas. Then a demand arose for vessels of a still higher character and this was met by building iron sailing vessels, which in time gave place to the present day Steamers.

The earliest mention of Sunderland as a Shipbuilding port dates from 1346, at which period Thomas Menvill had a place called Hynden (Hendon) for the building of vessels. Among the Mickleton MSS is a document which deals with Sunderland shipping from 1183 to 1609.

Wooden Ships In the days of wooden ships, the banks of the Wear, from the entrance to the harbour up to Hylton Ferry, were crowded with shipyards. Scarcely an opening on the shore of the river, or a nook or crevice in the limestone rocks which overhang it could be found, in which a ship was not in process of building. In the year 1801 there were nine shipyards; in 1814 the number had increased to twenty four. In 1833 there were thirty-four shipbuilding yards, and in 1840, when 251 ships were built, (the largest number for any year at Sunderland), there were no less than 65 shipyards employing 1600 shipwrights. To day there are 16 shipyards at Sunderland, but vessels are now built to carry 18,000 tons, (e.g. the "Algoa" built by Messrs. Doxford & Sons, Ltd.,) while in 1840 the average tonage of the ships was only 256 tons.

The ships were built of Oak, Beech, and Elm, with Baltic and American Pine for the decks, and African Teak, Mahogany, and Green Heart for cabin and other fittings. In 1753 there were 190 vessels belonging to our port and four of them were engaged in the Greenland Whale Fishery.

In 1815 there were 600 vessels with a total of 3,963 men and boys on board. Sunderland shipbuilders have long been famous for the strength and lasting qualities of their vessels. In 1772 the "Concord" a vessel of 168 tons was built on the Wear and for the long period of 79 years she ploughed the seas.

In 1851, when returning from the Baltic laden with timber, she encountered a terrific storm in the North Sea and was dismasted and waterlogged. In this condition she was picked up after the storm by a passing vessel, and towed into Scarborough. On the 4th of January, 1852 her hull was sold by auction for £391, amidst the cheers of the audience.

Mr. George Wilkin, a well known shipowner of Monkwearmouth, was the owner of the oldest vessel belonging to the port. This ship, named the "Blackbird," was eventually broken up, 100 years after it was launched.

In 1781, the frigate "Achilles," armed with twenty-eight guns was built at Sunderland, and in the following year, the frigate "Bucephalus" also carrying twenty-eight guns was launched.

These vessels were built by Mr. Thomas Dixon, of Monkwearmouth Shore, for James Stafford, Esq., and, as privateers, assisted the Naval Forces of the Crown in the Napoleonic Wars.

The launch of the "Lord Duncan," in 1796, from Southwick Quay, was long afterwards remembered as an important event. This was the largest vessel built in the port up to that time, and she could carry a cargo of 926 tons. She sailed on the 13th of July, 1798, for London where she remained unemployed until 1800, when she sailed for Smyrna and was taken into the Government service until August, 1802.

In 1806 she was chartered for the West Indies and was accidentally blown up at Port-au-Prince in 1807. By this unfortunate event Mr. William Havelock, the builder and owner, sustained a loss of upwards of £30,000. Amongst the smallest ships built at Sunderland may be mentioned one of three keels (63 tons) constructed in 1799 on Bishopwearmouth Green, by a shipwright in his leisure hours. When finished she was dragged to the river, a distance of about a mile, and launched.

Another of 15 tons was built in 1817, in a yard at the foot of Nile Street. She was taken on a wheeled carriage to the river and launched. She sailed for London with a crew of four men, and was sold to go to the West Indies in tow of a large ship, the "Janus." From this vessel she was parted in a storm, and actually arrived at her port three weeks before the "Janus." William Walker, the Captain of the little vessel, was a native of Sunderland.

Wear built ships have accomplished some of the quickest voyages on record. The "Chalmers" effected the voyage from Sunderland to Australia in 111 days and the "Vimiera" was only 86 days on her passage from London to Port Phillip. Both these fine sailing vessels were built by the late Sir James Laing.

Mr. William Pile, Jun., one of the most noted of wood shipbuilders on the Wear, was famed for the beautiful fast sailing China Clippers built in his yard. In 1851 he launched the "Chowringhee" of 1,000 tons. In 1852 the first iron ship built on the Wear, the "Amity," was launched from Laings' shipyard.

At different periods War Ships have been built on the Wear. In 1854 a Sunderland firm built 10 Gun Boats and two Mortar Boats for use in the Crimean War. The largest wooden ship ever built on the Wear was the "Duncan Dunbar" of 1,378 tons, built at Laing's yard in 1857.

In the same year the "Undaunted," an Auxiliary Screw Steamer, 1,244 tons, being also a full-rigged sailing ship, was built of wood by Mr. Robert James Brown. The auxiliary screw, when the vessel was under canvas, was lifted up the trunkway, out of the water, so as not to impede the vessel.

After 1860 the output of wooden vessels became less and less, until the last one, the "Coppenami," built by Messrs. William Pickersgill & Son, was launched on 22nd of April, 1880.

Ship- THE workmen in the shipyards, during the
wrights time of wooden ships, were called Shipwrights.

They were a steady and reliable body of men and were excellent workmen. The usual wage was 4/6 a day, and this was increased to 6/- a day in 1853.

The working hours were from six in the morning until six at night, with half-an-hour allowed for breakfast and one hour allowed for dinner. There were two Shipwrights' Union Societies in Sunderland and one of the rules imposed a fine of 5/- in the event of any member, at a meeting, uttering unlawful or disaffected expressions against the King or Government.

When the shipbuilding at Sunderland fell into a stagnant condition, between 1815 and 1822, a great many shipwrights were thrown out of employment and to lessen the distress the Shipwrights' Union commenced shipbuilding in the yard vacated by Mr. Thomas Tiffin. During this period many of the men obtained employment in the Government Shipyards, where Sunderland workmen were always cordially received and their work thoroughly appreciated. Several of the younger men went to sea in local vessels as ship carpenters.

Local A brief account of the sixteen shipyards on the
Ship- Wear is necessary, as no local history could
builders ignore this busy hive of skilled labour which
of has brought wealth and fame to our town.
To-day The shipbuilding firm of MESSRS. LAING & SONS is the oldest in Sunderland, having been established in the year 1793. This was the first

firm to introduce the novelty of a Floating Dock on the Wear. An old man-of-war, taken during the war with the Dutch, was purchased and converted into a very useful Floating Dock for repairing vessels. Atlantic Liners, Mail Boats, Twin-screw Passenger Mail Boats, Oil Steamers, and a new type of Trunk Deck Cargo Steamer are built by this firm. The works comprise machine shops, brass and iron foundries, and a special propeller foundry. The Admiralty contracts form a large portion of the work of this important yard. In 1918 five large vessels were launched by the firm in addition to Government Work.

The firm of MESSRS. S. P. AUSTIN & SON, LTD., was founded in 1826, and the business has passed through four successive generations of the family. The shipbuilding and repairing yards cover 6½ acres and have a river frontage of a quarter of a mile. In addition to a Graving Dock, 300 feet long, there is a fine Pontoon Dock capable of taking vessels up to 400 feet in length.

This well known local firm has a high reputation for building excellent vessels for general trades for British, Colonial and Foreign Shipbuilders. Last year four large vessels were launched and a considerable amount of work done for the Admiralty.

MESSRS. ROBERT THOMPSON & SONS, LTD., of the Southwick Yard and Bridge Dock Yard have been busily engaged in shipbuilding since the year 1834. The founder of the firm built the barque, "Iona" the first vessel to enter the North Dock at Sunderland when opened by Lady Williamson in 1836. How great has been the development of ships built by this firm since that 200 ton barque sailed into the North Dock, 83 years ago! The force of the contrast becomes appreciable when we visit the yard and note on the stocks the 5,000 and 6,000 tonners to which Messrs Thompson & Sons are now giving attention. Four large Cargo Steamers were launched in 1918.

MESSRS. R. A. BARTRAM & SONS hold a very prominent position amongst the shipbuilders and repairers of the port. The yards and workshops cover a large area of ground at the South Dock, and give employment to 800 workmen. The works are thoroughly equipped with powerful machinery of the most modern type, driven by electricity generated by Diesel Oil Engines. In addition to large cargo and passenger steamers the firm has had considerable experience in constructing vessels for the Admiralty. The late Mr. George Bartram, who was 91 years of age at the time of his decease, founded the business in 1836 in the days of wooden ships. About 50 years ago the firm began to construct steamers, and has since successfully carried out all the latest developments of this important industry, and played a most important part in establishing the high reputation of our town for shipbuilding. In addition to Government work Messrs. Bartram & Sons launched four large steamers in 1918.

The Pallion Shipyard, belonging to MESSRS. WILLIAM DOXFORD & SONS, was founded by the father of the late Sir W. T. Doxford in 1840. This is the largest and most important of the Sunderland Shipyards. Passenger and Cargo Steamers of the largest dimensions are constructed, including the Turret Class of cargo boat which can be seen in almost any port. For many years the firm has built war vessels for the Admiralty. On two occasions Messrs. Doxford & Sons have won the " Blue Ribbon" for shipbuilding by launching more vessels in a year than any other shipyard in the world. Everything required for steamers is made in the workshops, and their marine engines are unsurpassed. In 1918 Messrs. Doxford & Sons launched four torpedo destroyers and seven merchant ships.

The firm was amalgamated with the Northumberland Shipbuilding Co., in February, 1919.

MESSRS. JOSEPH L. THOMPSON & SONS have built ships at the North Sands Shipbuilding Yard since 1846. After launching, the vessels are taken to the Manor Quay Works, about ¼ mile higher up the river, where they are fitted with engines, etc. and made ready for the sea. This is one of the largest firms on the river with an extensive repairing business. A beautiful model of the S.S. "Euterpe," built for the Austrian Lloyds Steam Navigation Co., by Messrs. J. L. Thompson & Sons, may be seen in the model room of the local Museum. Seven steamers were launched last year.

The firm of MESSRS. W. PICKERSGILLL & SONS was established in 1847 by the late Mr. William Pickersgill, assisted by his sons William, Charles, and Frederick.

The firm soon acquired a high reputation for building fine wooden vessels. They followed up the changes from wood to iron and from iron to steel, building both sailing ships and steamers. The largest sailing ship constructed was the four master "Anderinah" at that period one of the largest British sailing vessels in the world. The number of men employed in this shipyard during normal times is about 1,000, and as a rule from five to six large high class steamers are built annually, mostly for British owners. Three vessels of a gross tonnage of 16,625 were launched in 1918.

The firm of MESSRS. SHORT BROS., PALLION, was commenced in 1849. The shipyard occupies 16 acres of ground and there are six berths capable of laying down vessels up to 700 feet long. The machines used in this establishment are all of the latest type, driven by electricity, and include their patent machine by means of which all the frame bars are "joggled." During the past 80 years Messrs. Short Bros., have built a large number of ships for local shipowners. In 1918 the firm launched six vessels, including the "Celtic Prince," which has a Board of Trade gross tonnage of 8,655.

MESSRS. JOHN BLUMER & Co., Iron and Steel Shipbuilders, was founded by the late Mr. John Blumer in 1859 and during the past sixty years, the firm has constructed vessels for every maritime nation in Europe, also for China, Japan, United States, etc., Mr. William Blumer, the son of the founder, is the head of the firm, and the steamers built in the North Dock Shipyard rank amongst the best constructed at the port. Four vessels were launched last year.

Three generations of MESSRS. J. CROWN & SONS, have built ships on the Wear, and although their shipyards have not been continually at work, yet there is a record for this firm of more than half a century's experience at Southwick and Monkwearmouth. The late Councillor J. Crown commenced building steamers at Monkwearmouth near the mouth of the river. He was also a well known repairer of ships, and on several occasions succeeded in getting shipwrecked vessels off the rocks on our coast, bringing them to his slipway, and making them again sea-worthy. Two vessels were launched last year.

MESSRS. OSBOURNE, GRAHAM & Co., have a large shipbuilding yard at Hylton, nearly four miles from the mouth of the Wear. Many fine vessels have been built by this enterprising firm since it was established in the year 1872. The well-known local vessel "City of Rochester," and the steamer "Virent"—one of the best equipped cargo vessels of the day, fitted with electric lights throughout, were constructed by the Hylton firm.

Messrs. Osbourne, Graham & Co., have also constructed vessels for the Admiralty, and large steam Hoppers and Dredgers for India and Holland. Three large steamers and two Naval Sloops were launched in 1918.

The shipbuilding and repairing works of THE SUNDERLAND SHIPBUILDING COMPANY, LTD., established in 1880, are situated at the South Docks. The firm has had a prosperous and successful career for 38 years, during this period constructing fine vessels for the Holland-America Line, the Blue Anchor Line, and for the well known London Shipowners, Messrs J. & C. Harrison. Newcastle firms have had many steamers constructed by the Sunderland Shipbuilding Company; repeated orders having been received from the Adam Steamship Co.; the Hall Bros. Co.; and the directors of the well known Prince Line. The firm has had considerable experience in building vessels for the Royal Navy.

Mr. C. J. Bewlay, the Managing Director, has been associated with the company for several years and the practical experience he gained with the Naval Construction and Armament Co., at Barrow; with Messrs. Armstrong & Mitchell, at Elswick; and as Manager of the Antwerp Shipbuilding Co.; has been of great value to the Sunderland Shipbuilding Co.

Three large vessels were completed in 1918.

The shipbuilding yard of MESSRS. JOHN PRIESTMAN & Co., is situated at Southwick and was established in the year 1882. It has made rapid progress and the Company is now regarded as one of the leading shipbuilding firms on the Wear.

In 1896 Mr. Priestman patented a Self-trimming Trunk Vessel, which has proved exceedingly successful and most economical. Numerous vessels of this type have been built during the last 23 years for British and Foreign Shipowners and several of them have been specially fitted for the cattle trade, each with accommodation for nearly 1,000 head of cattle.

The area of the yard and works cover about ten acres and the firm has every facility for constructing first class passenger and cargo vessels up to 600 feet in length.

Four vessels were completed in 1918.

MESSRS. SWAN, HUNTER, & WIGHAM RICHARDSON commenced shipbuilding at Southwick in 1917. The Southwick yard being a branch of the firms' establishments at Wallsend and Walker-on-Tyne, and as its output in 1918 (four vessels) is included with that of the other yards of the firm, making in all 29 ships, and gaining for the firm the Blue Ribbon for the United Kingdom, the Wear has a share in this honour.

During 1918 important developments on the river, as one of the great national centres of the shipbuilding industry, have taken place in the establishment at Pallion of the EGIS SHIPBUILDING CO.; and at Southwick of the yard of the WEAR CONCRETE SHIPBUILDING CO. Work in fitting out the sites and laying berths commenced during the early part of the year, and by July ships were in course of construction, steel cargo vessels at the Egis Shipyard and Concrete Ocean-going Tugs at the

Wear Concrete Works where the first concrete vessel has already been launched.

The chief shareholders of the Egis Yard are Sir John Ellerman, Sir William Gray, Lord Inchcape and Mr. Frank C. Strick. Three ships are in process of construction—one is an Admiralty B. Type standard vessel 400 feet in length and 52 feet beam, and will have a deadweight of 8,200 tons.* On the 1st January, 1919, the Egis Shipyard, Pallion, was amalgamated with the firm of Sir William Gray & Co., Hartlepool. When fully employed this new shipyard will contribute considerably to the local output of tonnage.

The building of reinforced concrete ships on the Wear is an important addition to the shipbuilding resources of Sunderland. The Concrete Yard is situated at Southwick on a portion of the riverside formerly known as the "Saltgrass." There is space for 7 or 8 berths for vessels up to 300 feet long.

Mr. Frank Forsyth, the Manager of the new yard has gained considerable experience abroad in the building of concrete ships, and it is anticipated that as the different moulds are now prepared the output of Standardised Vessels will be rapid.

CHAPTER XI.

THE COAL TRADE.

Early History   IT is the opinion of most historians that the Ancient Britons (prior to the invasion of the Romans), were familiar with the use of coal. Their flint and stone tools have been found at the "outcrops" of seams of coal in Durham and Monmouthshire. It has been proved that coal was worked

* This vessel, the "Golconda," was launched on 12th June, 1919.

partially by the Romans, not only by the discovery of their tools in disused coal seams, but coal cinders have also been frequently met with near the Roman Wall and among the Roman ruins at Lanchester and Ebchester in the County of Durham.

In A.D. 852, there is a record of the Abbey of Peterborough receiving twelve cart loads of fossil, or pit coal, and we know that Bishop Pudsey, in 1180, made a grant of land to a collier for providing coals for the cart-smith at Coundon, in the County of Durham. The smith at Bishopwearmouth, according to Boldon Book, held twelve acres of land for his service of making the iron work for the villagers' carts, etc., but in his case he had to provide his own coal.

The first Royal License was granted by Henry III, in 1239, to the Burgesses of Newcastle, to dig for coal, and in the year 1306, so general had its use become in London that the Parliament complained to the King, Edward I, that the air was infected, and in consequence proclamations prohibiting its use were issued. Nothing, however, resulted from this prohibition, as we find that in 1307 ten shillings worth of coals were used at the Coronation of Edward II.

In the year 1384, King Richard II granted leave to export the produce of the mines of the County of Durham, without paying any duties to the Corporation of Newcastle.

In 1396 coal was exported from Sunderland to Whitby and sold to the Abbot at three shillings and four pence per chaldron (53 cwts). Although ships conveyed coals from Sunderland before 1396 this is the earliest record we have at present. In 1609, during the reign of James I, Sunderland exported 11,648 tons and the average annual

THE COAL TRADE

export from 1704 to 1710 was 174,264 tons. During the war between Charles I and his Parliament, the port of Sunderland increased in importance from the circumstance that Newcastle had espoused the Royal cause and an embargo was laid on all ships in that port to prevent them supplying the City of London with coal. This led to a great increase of the coal trade from Sunderland to London. In 1642 Sunderland received a garrison from Parliament, and Sir William Armyne one of the Parliamentary Commissioners, resided here till the surrender of Newcastle in 1644. Through his influence in the year 1643, an ordinance of Parliament provided "that there be a free and open trade in the port of Sunderland, in the County of Durham, to relieve the poor inhabitants by reason of the rapines and spoyles these enemies of Newcastle have brought upon them, they being in great want and extremity."

It was not until the end of the eighteenth century that the three great obstacles which stood in the way of efficient coal-mining were removed. The invention of the steam engine in 1784 soon provided the means of keeping the mines clear of water, a system of ventilating the mines followed, and in 1815 the invention of the Safety Lamp removed many of the dangers due to explosions.

Year after year the coal trade increased until in 1820 the coal exported from Sunderland amounted to 1,115,812 tons.

From this date the River Wear Commissioners' returns show the combined exports of coal and coke, and the following table will show that the increased trade has been well maintained :—

1880	-	3,573,483 tons exported.
1890	-	3,740,330	,,
1900	-	4,262,095	,,
1913	-	4,857,661	,,
1914	-	4,074,589	,,

The Colliers and their Crews

THE wooden ships of the past, which carried the coal from Sunderland, were called "Colliers." They could carry from two keels (42 and two fifths tons), to twenty keels of coal. Our late townsman, Captain Edward Robinson, in his book called "Recollections of the Coal Trade," gives graphic descriptions of the ships, the crews, and the voyages they made. He thus describes the dress of the skippers—"When at sea their dress consisted of blue jacket and trousers, an old 'bell-topper' as the chimney pot form of hat was styled, neckerchief tied in a knot and twisted to the right or left of the neck, no braces to support the trousers, the striped shirt gracefully overlapping the trousers behind and before, and falling a little below the jacket and waistcoat. With a quid of tobacco on one side of the cheek and a ruddy, smutty, hardy, sea-beaten face, such was the rig of the collier skipper of the old school." Captain Robinson then goes on to describe the sailors—"When ashore they wore knee-breeches, and had their hair tied behind in a pig-tail. Black silk knee breeches were much worn. On Sundays blue swallow tail coats, with bright buttons, were almost the universal dress of the sailor. Blue cloth 'Tam o' Shanter' caps, with jacket, waistcoat, and trousers to match, were worn as evening dress, after coming ashore for the day, when work was done. On board ship canvas trousers were worn. Collier Jack prided himself in having the cut of a sailor. With his clean canvas trousers, worked and flowered in the front, blue jacket and waistcoat, long-quartered shoes, and striped shirt, with low crowned hat and pigtail, he was the very essence of all that constituted nautical correctness."

The Keels and Keelmen THE trade of the river in the past was carried on principally with Keels, which were all built with flat bottoms, so as to draw little water, on account of the shoals and caunches up the river. Each had a mast and a square sail but when a favourable breeze was lacking they were propelled by means of a long pole, called a set, which had a forked iron prong at the end. There were two methods of loading the Keels at Hylton. If the coal waggons were running the Keels would be loaded up direct from them, down a spout. The second method was to load them from the staiths long covered in sheds where the coal was stored. The Keel was laid against the quay wall, under the coal spout, and loaded by women and girls. Each woman had a barrow, a basket, and a shovel. When filled, the barrow was wheeled to the spout where it was emptied, and the contents slid into the Keel.

Each Keel was supposed to carry eight chaldrons, or a total of 21 tons 4 cwts. and this quantity still continues to be a keel of coals. About 700 keels were employed in conveying coals from the collieries on the bank of the river, to the ships in the lower part of the harbour. In addition to the Coal Keels there were also Ballast Keels, which carried from 50 to 60 tons. Each one was weighed and marked by the R.W.C., and licensed by them. The crew consisted of five hands and they would go alongside the collier, when she arrived, and discharge the ballast into the keel. The keelmen were paid according to the number of laden keels they discharged, so that their wages varied. Six men were usually engaged in "casting" a keel, and they received two shillings each for every keel they unloaded.

The keelmen were a brave and hardy class, and were frequently called upon to assist the work of our Navy. After the great Naval Victory at Copenhagen, in 1801, a number of Sunderland Keelmen assisted in the navigation of the captured Danish Ships to England. In 1803 some correspondence took place respecting the release of a number of Sunderland Keelmen who had been seized by the "Press Gang," and the Lords of the Admiralty intimated that unless the Keelmen of Sunderland provided men for the Navy, in the same proportion as the Newcastle keelmen (one in ten), they would still be liable to impressment.

The keelmen and casters were formerly a large and important element in the population of the town. For more than 200 years they had been the chief means of carrying on the principal trade of the port. In the year 1811, when the population of the town was 25,180, no less than 1,507 were keelmen, casters, or trimmers. As a race they were generally strong, thick set, and many of them tall, heavy men. Bowling on the Town Moor was a favourite pastime with them, and keel courses were also frequent. This was a race on the river between keels, each propelled by one man with the puy, or pole. The keelmen also, in their way, took a lively interest in passing events, and congregated in groups nightly at the street corners of the town end, where they discussed the various problems of the day.

In 1792 an Act of Parliament was obtained for incorporating the Keelmen on the Wear, and establishing a permanent fund for their relief and support in cases of sickness or for superannuation, and for widows and orphans, but the men did not take kindly to its provisions and the scheme was a failure. In Sunderland, as in other large towns, old customs and methods have given place to new and improved ones.

Steam ships, railway extensions, harbour improvements, and the invention of mechanical appliances for loading ships, have done away with the need for Keelmen, but we must never forget the important part they played in the early days of the coal trade.

CHAPTER XII.

THE WEAR POTTERIES.

The first vessels of clay, made on the banks of the Wear by the Ancient Britons, have already been described in Chapter I. They were all fashioned by hand, without the aid of the Potter's Wheel which was not used in Britain until the early iron age, about 500 B.C.

Roman Pottery THE remains of an ancient pottery were discovered during the excavations for the Sunderland Docks, in the year 1849. Whilst making the river entrance to the docks, it became necessary to remove the workshops of the Commissioners of the River Wear and to pull down some old houses occupying the Commissioners' Quay. Under these, the remains of what was considered to have been the site of a Roman Pottery were brought to light.

About eight feet below the surface appeared a circle, about twenty five feet in diameter, hewn out of the solid limestone rock. In the interior of this was a circle of

L

small rubble stone, in arrangement resembling a gin or horse-mill, which had apparently been erected for the purpose of grinding clay. Near this place was found a quantity of red and yellow ochre, and some broken earthenware, with four perfect specimens of Roman Bottles of common red unglazed ware.

One of the bottles was presented to the Newcastle Society of Antiquaries, and another, a very perfect one in all respects, was placed in the local museum.

Local Potteries of the Eighteenth Century THE first Sunderland Pottery of the Eighteenth Century was established by Mr. Phillips in the year 1750, and was known as the SUNDERLAND or GARRISON POTTERY. It stood on the site now occupied by the premises known as the " Pottery Buildings.' In addition to the ordinary printed ware, a large quantity of gold lustre ware and the well known figures of lions were manufactured by this firm.

The NORTH HYLTON POTTERY was founded in 1762, by Messrs. Maling Brothers. This was the first pottery in the north of England to introduce the process of printing pictures, etc., from copper plates, and transferring them to ware. This firm was noted for its lustre and enamel ware and for frog mugs. The latter were so called because in the interior of each mug was the figure of a frog, and when the mug was lifted up the frog appeared to the drinker as if about to leap down his throat. On one side of the mug was a view of Sunderland Bridge, and on the other side the words :—

> Tho' malt and venom seem united,
> Don't break my pot or be affrighted,
> For when it's full no spleen is seen,
> And when it's empty it's quite clean.

Mr. Antony Scott's SOUTHWICK POTTERY was built in 1788 and a very superior class of ware was made until the close of the works in 1897.

Another Southwick Pottery, founded in 1789 by John Brunton, was known as the WEAR POTTERY. Samuel Moore & Co., succeeded Mr. Brunton in 1803, and in 1864 it became the property of Mr. R. T. Wilkinson, Solicitor. Mr. Ralph Seddon, the manager of a large Staffordshire Pottery was then engaged and at his suggestions the small kilns were replaced by larger ones.

Improved machinery was also introduced, and from 1866 to 1872 the output of this pottery exceeded that of any other on the Wear. The net annual profit averaged £2,600. About 180 hands were employed and £7,000 were paid annually as wages. The Wear Pottery closed in 1874, when Mr. Seddon started the RICHMOND STREET POTTERY.

The SOUTH HYLTON or FORD POTTERY was erected about 1799 and work was successfully carried on by Messrs. John Dawson & Co., until 1864. This was a well-equipped pottery with the latest machinery and mills for grinding flints and colours. The "Willow Pattern" ware made by this firm was of a rich dark blue, and had a ready sale. Many interesting articles of earthernware were manufactured, including rose-coloured tea sets, gold, copper, and iron lustre ware. About 200 hands were regularly employed.

Local Potteries of the Nineteenth Century

MESSRS. T. J. Rickaby & Co., established the SHEEPFOLD POTTERY in 1840, for the production of Sunderland ware. This pottery is now carried on by Messrs. Snowdon & Co., who also work the BRIDGE END POTTERY which dates from 1845.

Mr. Wm. Burnside commenced a pottery in 1850, but it closed in 1858.

The DEPTFORD POTTERY was founded by Mr. Wm. Ball, in the year 1857. It continued to be noted for its excellent local ware, including fine tea sets, dinner sets, toilet sets, flower vases, and lustre ware, until it closed in 1918.

The last of the old potteries was Snowball's, HIGH SOUTHWICK POTTERY. This was noted for its brown ware, and two thousand four hundred articles were made weekly during the years 1869 to 1885.

Work in the Potteries AT the height of their prosperity about three thousand people were engaged in the local potteries. Men and women, boys and girls, found regular employment. There were apprentices serving seven years, and learning the art in each branch of the trade.

Women and girls attended every morning to buy the cracked and damaged goods as they came out of the kilns. These were then "hawked" about the town.

Keelmen brought the coal down the river from the Staithes above Hylton, and small sailing ships were chartered to bring white clay and stone from the South of England. These cargoes were discharged at the pottery quays by the help of cranes. Ships from France to Sunderland for coal were frequently ballasted with flints which found a ready sale at the local potteries at four shillings a ton. The flints were burnt in a kiln and afterwards ground to a powder in water. The grinding tubs were large round iron vessels paved with stones from Scotland. Four large iron arms were forced round by machinery and these arms pushed enormous stones round the inside of the vessel until the calcined flints were reduced to a cream-like substance which was then dried and used in the manufacture of earthenware.

Travellers were engaged to secure orders for the firms. They not only visited different parts of England but also made two journeys annually to the continent. Ships were engaged to carry the goods to London and other parts of the British Isles. Small vessels were chartered for the express purpose of carrying the ware to foreign countries, chiefly to Norway, Denmark, Prussia, and Holland. These vessels were always foreigners which had come to Sunderland for coal but accepted a better freight. It was a busy time at the pottery when a vessel was being loaded with ware. All the pottery workers assisted in carrying the goods to the ships while practised packers were busy storing the ware in the hold. It was no unusual thing for a small vessel to sail with a cargo valued at from £1,000 to £1,500 and to discharge the cargo without a single breakage. Over 300,000 articles of pottery were sent abroad annually from the Wear. In 1881 six hundred and eighty four crates of earthenware were exported. In 1891 there were only two hundred and twenty two, and in 1900 the number of crates had dropped to twenty six.

There have been no exports of earthenware from Sunderland since the year 1900.

The Decline of Local Potteries SEVERAL reasons have been given to account for the decline of the Wear Pottery Trade. Many skilled workmen were induced by offers of high wages, bonuses, and shares, to emigrate and teach the foreigners their art. This had such a disastrous effect on the home industry that an Act of Parliament was passed and any person found persuading British workmen to leave for a foreign country was subject to a fine of £500 or imprisonment for twelve months.

Having acquired the art of making earthenware, our foreign customers now became our trade competitors. They placed prohibitive tariffs on British goods, in order to secure their home trade and provide constant employment for their own countrymen, and at the same time they exported earthenware to Great Britain, where no tariff was charged on foreign manufactures.

Of late years our potters have been further handicapped by an influx of "dumped" goods from Germany and Austria. These goods being often sold at less than cost price are readily purchased by British people who have not realized that they are thus employing foreign instead of British workmen.

It is evident that the future strength and safety of the British Empire depends on our ability to produce what we require as largely as may be possible from our own soil and factories. We have allowed the foreigner to take quite a large share of the pottery trade and while we have kept a few types of ware, the foreigner has slipped in and wrested the remainder from us.

We have the necessary raw materials, reliable workmen, and only need the assistance of science to regain pre-eminence in this branch of manufacture.

Pottery in Local Museum
An hour or two may be spent profitably in examining the Ancient British, Roman, Greek, Maltese, Peruvian, Egyptian, and Mediæval pottery in our Museum, but the valuable collection of local ware exhibited is of special interest to Sunderland people.

It holds a worthy position in the history of the potter's art in this country, not perhaps especially as beautiful works of art, but rather as evidences to show the reflective person what our workers were a century ago. There is a maritime flavour about most of the poetry on the jugs and mugs which show that they were largely used by sailors, indeed, almost every sailor who visited our town in former days took home with him a set of Sunderland jugs, a frog mug, and a glass rolling pin, on which were depicted scenes from a sailor's life.

The following verse was very popular and may be seen on a lustre decorated jug and also on a punch bowl with portrait of Jack Crawford. :—

THE SAILOR'S RETURN.

Now safe returned from danger past,
With joy I hail the shore,
And fear no more the tempest's blast,
Nor ocean's angry roar.

The following lines inscribed on a butter dish are peculiarly full of human interest:—

When first I was a foremast man
I often did pretend,
That if e'er I got promoted
I would be a seaman's friend,
Then in a little time I was
Promoted to a mate,
But I then like all others
Soon forgot my former state.
When I became a Captain
I thought myself a king,
And very soon I did forget
The foremast man I'd been.

There is a fine collection of Sunderland Masonic Pottery in the Freemasons' Museum, London. Samples of fine Sunderland Ware are highly prized by collectors.

CHAPTER XIII.

THE SUNDERLAND GLASS TRADE.

Early History   SUNDERLAND may be regarded as the birthplace of the manufacture of glass in the British Isles.

The Venerable Bede, our first ecclesiastical historian, who was born at Sunderland in the year 672, relates that his contemporary, the Abbot Benedict, sent for artisans beyond the seas to glaze the windows of the Church and Monastery of Wearmouth.

By a singular coincidence, the first manufacture of window or crown glass in Great Britain, was established within a few miles of these monastic establishments.

In the year 1616, Admiral Sir Robert Mannsell erected glass works at Newcastle, which were carried on without interruption till nearly the middle of the nineteenth century, when they were closed. The history of the manufacture of glass at Sunderland, in the early part of the eighteenth century is obscure.

In Bishopwearmouth Church near the north door, leading into the nave, is the following inscription :—

Near this wall lies interred the body of
THOMAS WILSON,
One of the proprietors of the Glass Manufactory at
Ayre's Quay,
Who died the 30th November, 1776,
Aged 55 years.

Garbutt, in his History of Sunderland, states that there were seven bottle works and three glass works in 1817, and that 166 tons of manufactured glass were sent abroad in 1818.

The manufacture, as carried on so long in this locality, consisted of Plate, Crown, Sheet, Flint, and Bottle Glass. On the Wear alone there were at one time twenty-nine bottle making "houses," each of which had its own little army of busy toilers working the full six "journeys" a week.

Regular employment was also given to a fleet of small sailing ships which carried the products to London and the Continent. In the reigns of George III and George IV various Acts of Parliament were passed imposing heavy excise duties on the manufacture of glass, as well as placing the factories under the supervision of excise officers, who had to see to the observance of a series of complicated regulations under which the trade was carried on. In 1833 there were in Sunderland and South Shields eighteen glass manufactories, and these paid Government duty in that year to the amount of £133,196. With the removal of the duty and excise restrictions in 1845, a great impetus was given to the trade.

THE WEAR GLASS WORKS were founded by Mr. James Hartley and were the largest in the Kingdom. To Mr. Hartley is due the honour of inventing a new kind of plate glass called "rolled plate." The annual value of this glass made in Sunderland was £15,000. This glass was used extensively in the erection of the Crystal Palace in 1851. The firm was also noted for the manufacture of beautiful stained glass. A great improvement was made in this description of glass, inasmuch, as exterior staining of glass was superseded by glass made of the required tint in the crucible of the manufacturer. The glass therefore is not stained, but is inherently of its peculiar colour. This process of making coloured glass in the crucible has restored the art to its pristine state, for in such manner glass was made by the old masters.

Coloured glass from the Wear Glass Works was exported to all parts of the world. The firm also made immense quantities of sheet glass, and supplied one fourth of the amount required for the United Kingdom. Many of Mr. Hartley's workmen were famous for their exquisite workmanship, and articles of great beauty and elegance of design were constructed. Amongst these may be mentioned glass feathers, bird cages, cannon, bugles, hats, swords, and walking sticks.

Other workmen were experts in the art of glass cutting and engraving on glass. Tumblers, wine glasses, glass bowls and other articles were engraved with the owners' names and and also a view of Sunderland Bridge, with vessels sailing underneath.

The firm of Hartley played a conspicuous part in the Great Exhibition held in Hyde Park, London, in 1851.

The Exhibition Building itself was justly considered a triumph of the glassmaker's art and the Palace of Glass, or Crystal Palace, was afterwards provided with a permanent home at Sydenham. Messrs. Hartley & Co., showed numerous specimens of their manufactures, and in this section Mr. Hartley acted as one of the jurors.

Their exhibits comprised illustrations of glass manufactory commencing with a model (made in glass on a scale of $1\frac{1}{2}$ inches to the foot), of a glass making house with an eight pot furnace, and extended to a great variety of articles in successive stages of workmanship including ornamental and coloured glass.

Mr. James Hartley was highly respected in Sunderland; he manifested an active interest in the public

DECLINE OF THE GLASS TRADE

affairs of the town, and in 1842 was elected to the Council as the Representative of the West Ward. He was Mayor of Sunderland in 1851 and 1852, and one of the Parliamentary Representatives from 1865 to 1868. He retired from business in 1869 and died on the 2nd of May, 1886. The Wear Glass Works were finally closed in 1896.

Decline of the Glass Trade In the year 1864 the British Manufacturers of plate and window glass represented to the Government that the cost of their labour was sixty per cent more than that of their foreign rivals who were allowed to import their produce to this country *duty free*, whereas the Continental duties for British goods were prohibitory. No steps appear to have been taken to remedy this, and as a result the local glass trade steadily declined and the following old established works were closed and abandoned :—

1. Messrs. James Hartley & Co., Wear Glass Works.
2. Messsrs. P. Laing & Hubbard's, Ayre's Quay Wks.
3. Mr. Pemberton (succeeded by Mr. Kirk) ,,
4. Mr. Featherston's   -   -   -   ,,
5. Messrs. Horn & Scott's   -   -   ,,
6. Mr. Booth's Deptford Works.
7. Mr. Attwood (succeeded by Mr. Preston) Southwick Works.
8. Messrs. Fenwick & Co., Panns' Ferry Works.

A very large proportion of the plate and window glass now used in the United Kingdom is imported from foreign countries.

To restore the glass trade to our town it will be necessary to have improved machinery and improved methods. In America a group of six workmen make 16 bottles a minute ; in England a group of four workmen make 3 bottles a minute.*

Now if the American machinery and methods were adopted the British workmen would make more money, even if the present scale per gross was reduced one half, because they would make at least four times the quantity.

There are still five local glass works connected with our town. The two Southwick firms, Messrs. Alexander & Co., and Mr. T. Turnbull, employ about 700 hands and are chiefly engaged in the manufacture of patent screw-necked bottles, glass chimneys for lamps, tumblers, wine glasses, and other household glass ware. The remaining three firms are the Ayre's Quay Bottle Co., Messrs. Greener & Co., and Messrs. Hartley, Wood & Co. There has been a steady decline in the exports of glass and bottles from Sunderland during the past forty years. :—

In 1880 - 9,843 tons were exported.
  1890 - 7,822 ,, ,,
  1900 - 5,327 ,, ,,
  1913 - 3,442 ,, ,,
  1917 - 1,161 ,, ,,

CHAPTER XIV.

OTHER INDUSTRIES.

Marine Engines THE local works for the construction of marine engines are very extensive and complete, and the number of engines turned out annually not only supply all the requirements of steamers built at

* "Eclipse or Empire," page 272.

Sunderland, but many new vessels from neighbouring shipyards have their engines built at our port.

In addition to the local shipbuilders who make their own marine engines there are three large engineering firms in the town. MESSRS. GEORGE CLARK, LIMITED, is the oldest firm on the river Wear. Their works are situated at Southwick and the output exceeds twenty-five sets of engines annually.

The works of the NORTH EASTERN ENGINEERING CO., are situated on the east side of the South Dock, on land reclaimed from the sea at the time of the formation of the dock. In connection with these works is the large establishment at Wallsend-on-Tyne, and the two branches together form one of the largest marine engineering firms in the world.

The firm of MESSRS. RICHARDSONS, WESTGARTH & Co., has been formed by the union of the Scotia Engine Works, Sunderland, with Messrs. Thomas Richardsons, of Hartlepool, and Sir Christoper Furness, Westgarth & Co., of Middlesborough.

The amalgamation of the three firms took place in 1900, and the company has a high reputation as makers of marine and other engines.

Paper Making THE HENDON PAPER WORKS have been established for nearly fifty years, and give employment to about four hundred and thirty hands. Every description of paper is manufactured by this firm, and in addition to providing their customers in the United Kingdom, shipments are made regularly to all parts of the world. The firm makes two hundred tons of fine printing and writing paper, weekly. The principal raw material used is esparto grass, of which about 18,000 tons are imported annually.

The mills have their own electric lighting installation, and the motive power for the machinery throughout is steam.

The FORD PAPER WORKS have long been established on the river Wear. The firm have their own quay, where vessels discharge their cargoes of Esparto fibre into the warehouse direct from Africa.

The Lime Trade
AT one period Sunderland possessed a monopoly of the lime trade, being the only port from the Humber to the Forth engaged in this business. Lime kilns were to be found on both banks of the river as far as Claxheugh.

There were fifteen kilns at Pallion, belonging to Mr. Goodchild, and nearly 30,000 tons of limestone were converted into lime, annually. The lime kilns in Galley Gill, belonging to Bishopwearmouth Rectory, were under the management of Mr. Thos. Baker, and the lime was shipped at Galley Gill.

Fifty small vessels, of from forty to a hundred tons, were constantly employed in this trade in the past.

Large quantities were exported to Newport, on the Tees, Staithes, Whitby, Scarborough, and to several ports in Scotland. The limestone and lime from Sir Hedworth Williamson's Fulwell Quarries are now shipped from the North Dock.

Sunderland records of the past give particulars of manufactures and trades which are no longer carried on in the town.

Whale Fishing
DURING the years from 1753 to 1793, several vessels belonging to our port were engaged in the Greenland whale fishing. In 1790 Mr. Jos. Robinson purchased a large vessel and fitted her out as a whaler. The cargoes of blubber were boiled and

refined in a large building erected for the purpose on the top of the sea banks near the south end of the Barracks. John Berry was the owner and commander of the whale ship "Urania," and his brother William made many voyages to Greenland in local vessels.

Salmon Fishing MR. Taylor Potts in his History of Sunderland states "The most ancient commerce carried on upon the river Wear was the salmon fisheries. The Britons, the Romans, and the Saxons all seemed to have had the pleasure or sport of either spearing, netting, or otherwise catching the fish."

The Bishop of Durham leased the fishing rights, but the monks at Wearmouth, Finchale, and Durham had free fishing until the year 1358. The leases continued to be renewed, from time to time, for about three hundred years. The salmon were very plentiful in the river, and it is recorded that in 1788 a total of 72 salmon were taken in one draught near the mouth of the river. The lime, copperas, and other works on the river have driven the fish from the Wear.

Furriers IN 1807 Messrs. Richardson and Mounsey had a furrier's and canvas-weaving shop on the site of the old Roman Catholic Cemetery, between Queen Street and Cumberland Street, the latter being then called Factory Street. A large number of young women were employed at the works, and a good business was done in the manufacture of the popular beaver hats.

Iron Trade LONG before the Cleveland Hills were worked for iron ore, we were producing from the banks of the Wear, near Offerton and North Hylton, iron stone, iron boulders, or iron ore, and local vessels conveyed the mineral to the blast furnaces on the Tyne.

Grind- THE quarries at Cox Green and North Hylton
stones were noted for their grindstones which were
considered superior to any made on the Tyne.
In 1818, 4,000 whet stones and 936 tons of grindstones were exported to Europe and America.

Salt THE manufacture and trade in salt gave
employment to many people in former years.
The township of Wearmouth Panns derived its name from the ten salt panns, which were situated on the south side of the river, on the ground now occupied by Austin's shipyard.

Other articles made and exported one hundred years ago were :—Copperas, Charcoal, Lamp Black, Prussian Blue, Fire-bricks, Nails, Sail-cloth, Leather, Rope, and Boots and Shoes.

CHAPTER XV.

MEN AND WOMEN OF WHOM SUNDERLAND IS PROUD.

> Whene'er a noble deed is wrought,
> Whene'er is spoken a noble thought,
> Our hearts, in glad surprise,
> To higher levels rise.

> Honour to those whose words or deeds,
> Thus help us in our daily needs,
> And by their overflow,
> Raise us from what is low !   *Longfellow.*

Many brave Sunderland men have done gallant service for King and Country, and the town is justly proud of them. Not less do we admire and respect the memory of all those who have helped to bring prosperity and renown to our great seaport.

To BENEDICT BISCOP, the first Abbot of Wearmouth, we owe the churches at Monkwearmouth and Jarrow.

The VENERABLE BEDE, who was born at Sunderland in the year 672, and died at Jarrow in 735, will ever be remembered as our first historian and teacher. He devoted his life to the service of God and the welfare of his fellow-men. The beautiful stone cross at Roker was erected to his memory in 1904. (Further particulars of Bede and Biscop are given in Chapter III).

Among those who have fought for their King and Country may be mentioned the four sons of Mr. William Havelock, Shipbuilder, of Sunderland, who well deserve to be called the "Heroic Havelocks."

MAJOR GENERAL SIR HENRY HAVELOCK, K.C.B., was born at Ford Hall, on 5th April, 1795, and died in India, on 24th November, 1857. As the hero of Cawnpore and Lucknow, his renown is world-wide and his name will live in our annals for ever. A statue was erected to his memory in Trafalgar Square, London, and another in the Mowbray Park, Sunderland.

COLONEL WILLIAM HAVELOCK, K.H., entered the army in 1810, and distinguished himself by conspicuous bravery in Spain, France, and India, where he fell at the head of his regiment while charging the Sikhs at Ramnugger, on the river Cheenah, on 22nd November, 1848.

LIEUT.-COLONEL CHARLES FREDERICK HAVELOCK was engaged in every important battle in India for a period of twenty years. He possessed medals or clasps for Bhurppore, Ghuznee, Tezeen, Cabul, Moodkee, Ferozshah, Aliwal, Sobraon, and Goojerat. He died in his 65th year, on 14th May, 1868.

LIEUTENANT THOMAS HAVELOCK, the youngest son of Mr. William Havelock, served under Sir De Lacy Evans, in the British Legion against the Spanish Pretender, Don Carlos, and was killed in action in the service of Spain.

LIEUT.-GENERAL SIR HENRY HAVELOCK-ALLAN, K.C.B., V.C., was the son of Sir Henry Havelock, and his career as a soldier was almost as distinguished as that of his valiant sire. He entered the army when only sixteen years of age and served his country in India, Persia, Canada, New Zealand, and Egypt.

He took an active and prominent part in suppressing the Indian Mutiny, was three times wounded, repeatedly mentioned in despatches, and eventually won the Victoria Cross for personal valour at Cawnpore, in August, 1857. He was a Member of Parliament for Sunderland from 1874 until 1881 when he retired in order to take up a high military command at Aldershot. In March, 1880, he assumed the additional surname of Allan, by Royal License, having succeeded to the estates of the Allans of Darlington.

On the last day of the year 1897, the startling intelligence was published of the tragic death of this distinguished soldier, at the hands of the Afridis, in the Khyber Pass, North-West Frontier of India.

Sunderland Sailors have performed many deeds of bravery and played their part in all the great British naval engagements of the past. In 1820 the Committee of the House of Commons paid our sailors the following high compliment—"That the number of men obtained in the course of the war, from Newcastle and Sunderland, does not indeed bear a great proportion to the whole of the men employed and raised in the same time for the navy; but their value is not altogether to be estimated by their numbers. The difficulties of the navigation in the coal-trade are admitted to give the seamen, derived from it, in point of skill and experience, patience of fatigue and hardship, an incontestable superiority over those drawn from other maritime trades of the kingdom."

In point of prowess and personal valour, the sailors of the port of Sunderland stand as high as any belonging to neighbouring ports.

In the memorable engagement which Admiral Lord Duncan had with the Dutch Fleet off Camperdown on the 11th of October, 1797, the flag of the "Venerable," Lord Duncan's ship was shot away by the Dutch Admiral De Winter. JACK CRAWFORD, a Sunderland sailor, immediately ran up the shrouds, with a mauling spike in his hand, and, with the greatest coolness and intrepidity, nailed the flag to the top-gallant-mast head. For this heroic and daring action he was awarded a pension of £30 a year, and his fellow townsmen, in testimony of his heroism, presented him with a silver medal which may be seen in our Museum. The statue on Mowbray Park was erected to his memory in 1890.

Another heroic instance of valour was displayed by CAPTAIN HORNSBY and his crew, on board the "Isabella," of Sunderland. The crew consisted of five men and two boys, and the vessel carried four guns and two swivels. While steering for the Hague, she fell in with the Marquis of Brances, a French privateer with a crew of 75 men and armed with ten guns and eight swivels. After a long contest the French vessel was sunk and all her crew, except three, perished. King George III presented Captain Hornsby with a large gold medal for his bravery.

JOSEPH R. HODGSON was born at Bishopwearmouth on 3rd of October, 1829, and died at London in Nov., 1908. When only twelve and a-half years of age he saved the life of a child, who had fallen into the river Wear, and on other occasions he saved twelve people from drowning, and rescued by his personal efforts the crews of 16 vessels wrecked upon the Sunderland coast. It is computed that he saved upwards of 200 lives. He was known in Sunderland as "The Stormy Petrel." In 1857 he received a massive gold medal from Napoleon III for rescuing the crew of the French vessel "The Three Sisters." In 1883, his fellow townsmen presented him with a second gold medal and at other periods he was awarded five silver medals for his heroic deeds. Arrangements are being made to purchase the medals and place them in the Museum.

The deeds of the "Stormy Petrel" rank high among the daring actions of Sunderland men, and his memory will never be forgotten in his native town.

HARRY WATTS, another local hero, was born on 15th of June, 1826, and was apprenticed as a sailor before he was fourteen years of age.

After twenty-two years of sea faring life he was appointed as a diver to the River Wear Commissioners. He was the means of saving thirty-six lives; the first before he was fourteen years of age and the last when he was in his 66th year.

Mr. Watts presented his eight medals and six certificates awarded to him for life saving, to the Sunderland Corporation and they are now deposited in the local Museum.

Mr. Andrew Carnegie, the donor of the three Branch Libraries which Sunderland possesses, had an interview with Harry on the 21st of October, 1909. He was delighted with the old hero and awarded him a pension of £60 a year. Harry Watts died on 26th of April,

1913, and his pension is continued for the benefit of his widow during her lifetime.

As an example of courage and great kindness an incident in the career of the late CAPTAIN STEPHEN RACKLEY may be recorded. Captain Rackley had a record of fifty-two years service in the Sunderland Lambton Colliery ships. He was at Hamburg with his vessel on the occasion of the great fire in 1842. Together with his officers and crew he assisted in subduing the flames and rescuing the people from the burning houses. He afterwards accommodated a large number of women and children, who were homeless, on board his vessel. For his prompt assistance and kindness he was presented with the freedom of the City of Hamburg, together with a commemoration medal, cast from the Cathedral bells, which were damaged by the fire. Capt. Rackley died at Sunderland in 1903 in his eighty-eighth year, and he will long be remembered for his many sterling qualities and his genial disposition.

DOCTOR CLANNY, the inventor of the Miner's Safety Lamp, resided in Sunderland for many years and took an active interest in the welfare and progress of our town. In 1804 he was elected a member of the Sunderland Subscription Library, and in 1816 he was awarded the silver medal of the Society of Arts for the "Clanny Safety Lamp." In the following year the Society presented him with a gold medal for inventing the "Steam Safety Lamp." The Durham coal owners, in 1845, presented him with a piece of silver plate as an acknowledgment of his eminent services in the causes of humanity and science. Dr. Clanny died on the 10th January, 1850, and was buried in the old Gill Cemetery. There is a fine oil painting of Dr. Clanny in the Town Hall.

WILLIAM SHIELD, musician, was well known and respected in our town. He was famous as a composer and wrote the music for Burns' well known song " Auld Lang Syne."

He was honoured with a public funeral in Westminister Abbey.

SAM ROXBY and JOHN EMERY were well known Sunderland Actors of the past. Natives of the town who have made a name in our literature included the well known TOM TAYLOR, author, and editor of Punch ; GEORGE WILSON MEADLEY, and PROFESSOR HOLMES.

Two favourite writers on local subjects were CAPTAIN EDWARD ROBINSON, Author of "Recollections of the Coal Trade," "Life of Jack Crawford," etc., and JOHN GREEN, the Author of "Tales and Ballads of Wearside."

We must not forget LAWRENCE GOODCHILD, the Blind Poet and Scholar, who was born at Sunderland in 1813. The following lines, from his poem "Hoel," published in 1835, are worthy of more than a passing thought when we remember our brave townsmen who fought recently in France and Flanders.

"Then fear not, ye Britons, to rush on the foe,
If triumphant, for ever your triumph shall glow ;
If ye perish, ye perish your country to save,
And never shall fade the renown of the brave."

The undaunted courage in face of danger which has always been manifested by our local heroes of the past, was shown by the members of the present generation when taking part in the great struggle on the Continent (1914 to 1918).

As an example we give the place of honour to our townsman LIEUTENANT GEORGE MALING, who won the

Victoria Cross for the noblest kind of bravery shown in battle. The following is a copy of the official account :—

"During the heavy fighting near Fauquissart, on the 25th of September, 1915, Lieutenant Maling worked incessantly with untiring energy from 6-15 a.m. on the 25th until 8 a.m. on the 26th collecting and treating in the open air, under heavy shell fire, more than 300 men. At about 11 a.m. on the 25th he was flung down and temporarily stunned by the bursting of a large high-explosive shell, which wounded his only assistant and killed several of his patients. A second shell soon after covered him with debris, but his high courage and zeal never failed him and he continued his gallant work singlehanded."

The gifted artist, CLARKSON STANFIELD, R.A., was a native of our town. He died in 1867 and was buried in Westminster Abbey. There is a mural tablet in the entrance hall of the Museum and Art Gallery, erected to his memory. Other well known Sunderland Artists were JAMES STOKEL, W. CROSBY, MARK THOMPSON, and RICHARD HALFNIGHT.

There are eleven beautiful paintings by the above Artists in the Art Gallery.

Copy of Tablet in Museum and Art Gallery Hall :—

CLARKSON STANFIELD, R.A., R.S.A.,
Was born in Sunderland High Street, on 3rd of December, 1793, and died on the 18th of May, 1867.
"The leader of English realists, and incomparably the noblest."
J. Ruskin.

His Father,
JAMES FIELD STANFIELD,
A lover of liberty, and an accomplished scholar,
Founded the first Literary and Philosophical Society
in Sunderland.
Died 15th of May, 1824, Aged 74.
Father and Son were citizens of the Town and Borough
of Sunderland.

By Public Subscription, A.D. 1900.

There have been many noble and generous hearted women, natives of Sunderland, whose names should ever be remembered.

In 1699 DAME DOROTHY WILLIAMSON, widow of Sir Thomas Williamson, Baronet, provided a sum of money, the interest of which is paid annually, for ever, to the poor of Sunderland and district.

In 1725 MRS. JANE GIBSON, widow, of Sunderland, left £1,400 to provide homes for twelve poor people. These homes are situated near Bishopwearmouth Church.

In 1778 MRS. ELIZABETH DONNISON, widow, left £1,500 for the purpose of founding a Perpetual School for teaching poor girls belonging to the Parish of Sunderland. The school is situated near Sunderland Church.

In 1820 MRS. WOODCOCK established the Marine Alms Houses in Crow Tree Road, for the reception of ten widows or unmarried daughters of Master Mariners.

She also gave £1,000 to the Sunderland Parochial School; £1,000 to the Bishopwearmouth Parochial School; and £600 to the Shipwrecked Mariners' Society.

Mrs. Woodcock died at Cheltenham on the 20th of March, 1841, aged 80 years. She was a liberal patroness to the institutions of her native town (Sunderland) and her private charities were also extensive. The poor always found in her a kind benefactress, and no appeal to her benevolence was ever made in vain.

THE SUNDERLAND FLORENCE NIGHTINGALE.

On the 26th of October, 1831, the disease called Cholera Morbus made its appearance in this country at the port of Sunderland. So fatal were its effects, that between the 26th of October, 1831 and the 3rd of April, 1832, there were 538 people suffering from the disease, of whom 205 died.

A noble woman, whose name is worthy to be classed with Florence Nightingale's, volunteered to nurse the poor sufferers at the hospital. The following is a copy of the epitaph on her tombstone which may be seen in the old Sunderland Churchyard :—

SARAH FAIRLEY,
Nurse at the Sunderland Hospital for Cholera Patients,
A.D. 1831,
Who sacrificed her life in the endeavour to save
the lives of others.
" I was sick and ye visited me."

THE SUNDERLAND GRACE DARLING.

Many years ago a well known family living at the Mark Quay rendered gallant service, on many occasions, when people were in danger of being drowned in the Wear.

Mr. Fairley, his wife, and two sons, had always a boat ready for immediate use and the four members of this family were the means of saving more than twenty persons from drowning.

The late Mrs. Fairley not only assisted in rescuing many people, but also rendered valuable services in attending to the injuries of those who had been saved. The past generation of inhabitants of the river-side greatly respected and honoured Mrs. Fairley and regarded her as the Sunderland Grace Darling.

CHAPTER XVI.

SUNDERLAND IN 1918.

Sunderland, the largest and most important town in the County of Durham, is a County Borough and a Parliamentary constituency returning two members. The town is governed by a Mayor, 16 Aldermen, and 48 Councillors. It is essentially a business town, its most important industries being all connected with shipping.

From 1914 to 1918 the trade of the Port was below the average. This will be seen by comparing the River Wear Commissioners returns for the years 1913 and 1918.

PRINCIPAL IMPORTS.

	1913.	1918.	
Timber	54,673	10,895	Loads.
Props	41,091	4,079	,,
Iron and Steel	9,158	3,851	Tons.
Ores	139,971	68,809	,,
Chalk, Loam, &c.	35,248	3,083	,,
Grain	312,201	140,835	Qrs.
Esparto Grass	19,957	1,056	Tons.
Wood Pulp	977	- -	,,
Petroleum	42,616	7,036	,,

PRINCIPAL EXPORTS.

Coal & Coke	4,857,661	2,062,061	Tons
Bottles & Glass	3,442	- -	,,
Lime	958	- -	,,
Iron & Steel	7,228	- -	,,
Cement	31	- -	,,
Pitch	20,720	7,621	,,
Creosote Oil	13,582	1,118	,,

Chief Buildings Many fine public and private buildings have been erected in Sunderland during the past 50 years, and three Public Parks have been opened during the same period. Other noticeable and recent improvements include the erection of the Queen Alexandra Bridge; the introduction of the Electric Light and Electric Trams; and the opening of the New Docks. Fawcett Street, once devoted entirely to private residences, is now the chief business centre and contains the Town Hall, the Subscription Library, five important Banks and handsome Shops and Offices. This street is considered to be one of finest business streets in the North of England.

Very stately examples of architecture may be seen in the New Offices of the River Commissioners, the Sunderland and South Shields Water Company, and the Sunderland Gas Company, while the banking establishments of Barclay & Co., Bank of Liverpool, Lloyds & Co., London City and Midland, London Joint Stock, and the National Provincial have added considerably to the appearance of the business streets of the town.

The Town Hall The Town Hall is our finest public building and was opened on 6th November, 1890. It has frontages in Fawcett Street and Athenæum Street. The most conspicuous exterior feature is the Clock Tower, 140 feet high, 20 feet square, and finished at the top with a cupola dome and lantern, forming one of the chief landmarks in Sunderland. The clock has four illuminated dials of cast-iron skeleton frame, each eight feet six inches in diameter, to form the circles, figures and minutes; each dial is filled with white opal glass. The principal entrance is in Fawcett Street, the arched doorway having on either side dwarf pillars supporting a balcony with a fine central window. On the first floor are the Council Chamber, the Mayors' Parlour, and the Reception Room. All the interior arrangements are excellent. On the wall of the first floor corridor is the tablet containing the names of local Volunteers who were made Freemen of Sunderland in honour of their services in the South African War. The whole of the second floor is devoted to the School of Art, while other rooms are for the use of the Town Clerk, the Borough Surveyor, the Rate Office, the Health Department, etc.

The total cost of this fine building was £45,000.

The Public Library, Museum, and Art Gallery
THESE imposing premises were erected from the designs of Messrs. J. and T. Tillman, at a cost of about £12,000, the foundation stone being laid on September 28th, 1877, by Alderman S. Storey, then Mayor, in the presence of General Grant, Ex-President of the United States. The building was opened on November 6th, 1879. The entrance hall contains many objects of interest: the Library and Art Gallery entrance being on the right, and that to the Museum on the left.

The Library is a spacious well-lighted room, containing some 28,000 volumes. The average daily circulation of books is 1,300, and each year many new volumes are added. There is a reading room for ladies, but there is no reference room owing to congestion. The three branch libraries, the gift of Mr. Carnegie, are situated at Monkwearmouth, Hendon, and Millfield; and each contains about 8,000 volumes. These were the first libraries in the North to be organised on the "open access" system.

The Museum contains over 35,000 specimens which may be classed as follows :—Natural History, Antiquities, Ethnology, and Technology. The first section is rich in mammalia, birds, insects, and shells; there are also Canon Norman's and other British Herbarium; large collections of minerals and fossils, and collections illustrating the botany, geology, and zoology of the County of Durham. The remaining sections consist of stone and bronze implements, local pottery, and models of locally built ships, etc. The Earl of Durham presented an entomological collection of about 3,000 specimens, brought together by the first Earl, while Governor-General of Canada.

There is an exceedingly fine collection of British birds, which, excepting some rare specimens, is complete. Recently the nests and eggs of many of the birds have been added. Pehaps one of the most interesting exhibits is that of fossil, mineral, and rock specimens from Sunderland and district.

This collection, with photographs and geological maps, is of great local value.

There have been numerous gifts to the Museum; a valuable collection of Natural History specimens and Antiquities, collected by the late Mr. Edward Backhouse, is one of the most recent presentations. The chief items consist of 6,000 butterflies; 4,000 finely preserved British and foreign shells, including many of rare varieties; 1,500 geological specimens; 600 flint implements and numerous botanical and ethnological specimens, and objects of antiquarian interest. This collection, which is in beautiful condition and of great educational value, is one which any town might be proud to own. It is fully recognised that the Museum plays an important part in Education. There are frequently special exhibitions as:— photographs of famous modern pictures, collections of local prints, exhibition of art work from Local Council Schools, illuminated manuscripts and loan exhibitions from South Kensington. The Museum is being frequently visited by parties of scholars and their teachers, from local and neighbouring schools to study or to draw various exhibits.

Great interest has been aroused in practical experiments originated by Mr. J. A. Charlton Deas, Curator and Head Librarian of Sunderland ; these taking the form of showing some of the content of the Museum and Art Gallery to the local adult and juvenile blind, through the sense of touch. These experiments which are full of intense interest, are described in the Library Circulars Nos. 55 to 60, and in the Museum Journal Vol. 13. These experiments are now a permanent feature in a number of Museums throughout the World.

The Art Gallery THE Local Art Gallery contains a permanent collection of ninety-seven British and Foreign Oil and Water-colour Paintings, together with several specimens of sculpture, including a cast of the famous " Athlete struggling with a Python," by Lord Leighton.

In 1908 a handsome gift of thirty-one pictures from the late Mr. John Dickinson, J.P., enriched the collection. The works are nearly all by well known British Artists of the Victorian era.

Annually four loan exhibitions of paintings, photographs, engravings, etc., are shown on screens, and evoke much interest.

One of the greatest educational needs of Sunderland to-day is an extension of the Library, Museum and Art

THE VICTORIA HALL

Gallery. The former is without a Reference Room, and the two latter have not space to display nearly all their treasures to advantage. There are four hundred fine engravings belonging to the town and no suitable place to exhibit them. As the rate for supporting these institutions is limited by the Act under which it is levied, to three half-pence in the pound, it will be seen that the only hope of realising the much needed extension must, as in the case of more fortunate towns, depend on the private munificence of some prominent citizen interested in the welfare of Sunderland.

The Victoria Hall THIS fine building, the largest public hall in the town, with accommodation for three thousand people, is pleasantly situated in Park Terrace, facing Mowbray Park. It was erected in 1872 at a cost of nearly £13,000, in 1901 it was sold to the Sunderland Corporation for £8,000, and some years later under the direction of Mr. Eltringham, Architect, the hall was considerably increased in size, and the interior greatly improved by the addition of two small halls for banquets, balls, etc.

The dining hall has accommodation for two hundred and twenty, while the small hall or ballroom will hold for meeting purposes seven hundred people.

The total cost of this public building, which is considered to be one of the finest public halls in the North, was £36,305, inclusive of extension, alterations and fittings.

Technical College THE Technical College was opened on Sept. 13th, 1901 ; the total cost, about £28,000, being met by the accumulated subsidy received under the Local Taxation Act, and by a loan of £10,000 which was raised on the security of the Borough Fund.

The opening of the College marked another forward step in the progress of Educational equipment of the town, and made provision for a sound technical training in the shipbuilding, engineering, mining, agricultural and other industries of Sunderland and district.

In 1902, the local shipbuilders, engineers, etc., subscribed £3,000 for the further equipment of the engineering and mechanical laboratories.

The affairs of the Technical College are administered by a body of Governors, partly selected from members of the Education Committee, and partly of co-opted members. The Principal is Mr. V. A. Mundella, M.A., B.Sc.

New Police Station, Courts, etc. A fine block of buildings was opened in Gill Bridge Avenue in 1907, to accommodate the Court of Quarter Sessions, Police Court, and the Fire Brigade Station. It is an imposing structure, stone-built, surmounted by a large clock tower, and providing apartments for the Chief Constable, Magistrates, Magistrates' Clerk, the Recorder, the Clerk of the Peace, as well as Counsel's retiring rooms and waiting rooms. This new building, in which all the different branches of the local police establishments are now concentrated, near the centre of the town, was erected at a cost of over £40,000.

Chief amongst our local philanthropic institutions are the Royal Infirmary and the Children's Hospital, both in Durham Road; the Sunderland and Durham County Eye Infirmary in Stockton Road; the Monkwearmouth and Southwick Hospital; the Royal Institute for the Blind; the Orphan Asylum; the Nursing Institute; the Waifs' Rescue Agency and the Home for old people known as the Little Sisters of the Poor.

The Royal Infirmary

THE Sunderland Infirmary, like many another useful institution, began its career in very humble circumstances. It has, however, happily for suffering humanity, not only held on its way, but has grown with the growth of the town, and the magnificent group of buildings in the Durham Road, which it now presents, is a sure proof of the hold it has on the hearts of Sunderland people.

The foundation stone of the first Infirmary in this town was laid on January 10th, 1822, by the Right Hon. Lord Stewart, afterwards Marquis of Londonderry. The building, only consisting of two storeys with accommodation for nineteen patients and twelve beds for fever cases, was erected at a cost of £3,000. The old site is now occupied by the Catholic School in Chester Road. In June 1855, a free accident ward was opened "for the admission of all persons whether labourers, artizans, or sailors (not being paupers), happening an accident which might render them unable to follow their employment and who were not in circumstances to afford the employment of such assistance at their own homes." From 1823 to 1860, the institution did much good work and increased its responsibilities. As Sunderland was now growing in size and population, the committee had once more to seek new and larger quarters. In February, 1864, land was purchased for the new site on the Thornhill Estate, Durham Road. In September of the same year plans were prepared by Messrs. Potts and Sons; these were approved and before long building operations were in progress. The opening ceremony took place on December 26th, 1867, when Earl Vane was present. As years passed and the need arose new wings were erected. The portion of the building called the "Backhouse

Memorial Wing," in memory of the late Edward Backhouse, Esq., always a warm supporter of the Infirmary, was erected in 1882.

In 1892 the isolation block, the cost of which was defrayed by Miss Foster, was completed. In the same year a Convalescent Home, the Heatherdene Home, was opened at Harrogate. The year 1900, saw a new wing, costing £15,000, erected, thus showing how the building was growing apace. In 1898, a new Home for Nurses was erected in commemoration of Queen Victoria's Diamond Jubilee. The good work of this institution, now known as "The Royal Infirmary," is endless and far-stretching. All classes of the inhabitants of Sunderland contribute to its needs but one gives special mention to the local workmen who contribute over £6,000 annually.

The Eye Infirmary THIS institution began in a very small way in the East-end of Sunderland in 1836; it was originated by two medical men, the late Mr. E. H. Maling and Mr. Dodds. The majority of the patients were "out-patients" and the subscriptions were very small. As in the case of the Royal Infirmary the premises were soon too small, and in 1881 the institute was moved, this being for the third time, to Crow Tree Road. The present building was opened in 1893 in Stockton Road, and is regarded as one of the best eye infirmaries in the kingdom. Some 7,000 cases, including over 500 operations, are dealt with every year. The present site is too small for the large number of cases treated, and a new site known as the Bede Tower has been bought in Burdon Road. The Sunderland and Durham County Eye Infirmary is supported by voluntary subscriptions to which the workmen of our town generously contribute.

The Children's Hospital THE Children's Hospital, one of the most pleasing of Sunderland's fine buildings, was officially opened on May 29th, 1912. Great pressure of work on the Royal Infirmary decided the committee to build a separate hospital for children, and so leave more accommodation for adults in the main institution. Mr. John S. G. Pemberton gave two acres of land on the Barnes Estate, in memory of his father the late Mr. Richard L. Pemberton. As the two acres of land were not sufficient the committee purchased two more. The Hospital was built by Mr. J. Huntly, Contractor, from plans prepared by Messrs. W. & T. R. Milburn, Architects. The building consists of a central two-storey block, with a pavilion on either side, the whole scheme carried out in red brick which gives it an imposing and cheerful appearance.

One pavilion has been named "The Gordon Pavilion," in memory of the late Mr. Frederick Gordon, J.P., the other is "The Priestman Pavilion," in memory of the late Mrs. John Priestman. The lecture hall is the gift of Miss Arkell and past and present pupils of Claremont House School, and certain named cots are supported by various religious institutions.

The Durham County Royal Institute for the Blind THIS institution was founded in 1877, by Miss Ada M. Byers, and provides employment for some 60 blind people. The following articles are made in the workshops at Villiers Street:—baskets, mats, brushes, wicker chairs, cushions, also mattresses and other upholstery for ships and steamers, and in addition hair mattresses are re-made and re-covered, and chairs re-caned.

There are two ways in which the inhabitants of Sunderland may help this deserving institution. The first is by contributing directly to the funds, and the second is by purchasing the things needed for the home which can be obtained there. This would enable the Manager to provide more employment, as at the present time many of the workers cannot be fully employed.

Sunderland Orphan Asylum This excellent institution was established by Act of Parliament in 1853, and provides a home for about 50 boys. Its doors are open to the orphans of seafaring men from any part of the Kingdom. Though it has a small endowment it depends chiefly for its support on voluntary contribution. Candidates for admission are elected by the votes of the Principals, Governors, and Subscribers.

FINE WAR RECORD.

The Sunderland Orphan Asylum has a war record of which it has every reason to be proud.

Of the lads trained at the school over 120 have joined either the Navy or the Army. They include a sub-lieutenant and a first-class petty officer in the Navy, while in the Army the school is represented by four second-lieutenants, one quartermaster-sergeant, one sergeant-major, nine sergeants, and ten corporals. One lad gunner, James Trott, has been awarded the Military Medal for conspicuous bravery, eighteen have given their lives for King and Country, and thirty-two have been wounded or invalided from the front.

Seven of those in the mercantile marine have been in torpedoed vessels, one lad was drowned, but all the rest joined other vessels at the first opportunity.

The Old Boys who have fallen in the War are as follows :—

Sub-Lieutenant Arthur Burlinson.
Seamen Harry Clark and Jack Crawford. Apprentice James Mordey.
Corporal William Lowes (Canadians), and Lance-Corporal Alfred Ranton.
Gunners Thomas Orwin, and John Ranton.
Rifleman William McLachlan and Bandsman Tom Rooks.
Privates Richard Duncan, George Hagedorn, Fred Finley, Charles Chapman, Richard Lamb, Robert Peverley, George Milburn (Australians), and R. Clifford Singleton (Canadians).

Since the school was opened on October 17th, 1861, (58 years ago), 560 boys have been trained and educated within its walls. Of the success of their training the honour boards in the dining-hall bear witness, including as they do the names of school-masters, captains, mates, sea-going engineers, draughtsmen, officers of the Board of Trade, mine manager, pilots, relieving officers, etc.

In November of each year since 1904, the Old Boys have forwarded contributions to their Old Boys' Fund towards the support of the school which has done so much for them. The average amount for the past 13 years was £24-0-11, or a total of £313-0-11.

George Hudson Charity THE late Mr. George Hudson, Shipowner, left the sum of £164,234 to be invested for the purpose of assisting and educating orphan children. The fund has been adminstered since 1884, by a Committee of Trustees, and 270 children are receiving the benefit of the Charity.

THE MONKWEARMOUTH AND SOUTHWICK HOSPITAL, founded in 1873, is situated in Roker Avenue, and may be regarded as the Royal Hospital for Monkwearmouth and district.

THE DISTRICT NURSING ASSOCIATION was established for the purpose of providing nurses to attend to the sick poor in their own homes, free of charge.

The home for old people situated in Chester Road, has accommodation for about 200 inmates and is under the management of a Roman Catholic Sisterhood, called the "LITTLE SISTERS OF THE POOR."

Education THE first elementary schools in Sunderland were erected in 1808, and were known as Parochial Schools. They were supported by voluntary contributions and the school fees were one penny weekly from each pupil. In 1833 Parliament for the first time gave a grant in aid of education. In 1851 there were 24 public schools and 120 private schools, three of the latter being successful secondary schools of the type conducted by the late Dr. Cowan, at the Grange.

These 144 schools were attended by a total of 8,516 children, the estimated number of children of school age in the town being 15,000.

The Grange School THE Grange was a private school, conducted by the late Dr. James Cowan. There were about 160 boarders, principally from the North of England and Scotland, and a considerable number of day scholars from Sunderland and district. Many pupils from this school attained high rank in their respective professions, namely : Lord MacNaghton (who became a Lord of Appeal), Bishop Sandford, Lord Sandford, Lord Sinclair, Sir David Baird, Sir John McNeill, Bart., Sir Robert Anstruther, Bart., Hercules Ross, (Indian Civil Service, and celebrated rifle shot), Major-General Maxwell, Capt. Shaw, V.C., Lieut. Cadwell, V.C., Sir Montstewart Grant Duff, etc. Sunderland pupils included Tom Taylor (an Editor of "Punch"), Sir James Laing, Bart., E. Capper Robson (Solicitor), and his brothers Hugh and John, W. Grimshaw, Dr. Welford, John Harrison, Henry Stobart, W. J. Young

(Solicitor), Arthur Dixon, Henry Dixon (Solicitor), Jos. Brown (Solicitor), Rev. C. S. Collingwood, William Ritson, John Graham, and many others. Dr. Cowan retired in 1846. Of the numerous pupils educated in the Grange School there only remains our distinguished townsman, Mr. John Graham, Coroner, and Deputy-Lieutenant of the County of Durham.

Since the passing of the Education Act of 1870 the educational facilities of Sunderland have been worthy of the position and prestige of the borough. There are to-day 32 elementary schools (provided and non-provided) with accommodation for 30,105 pupils and having 28,266 names on the rolls. These schools are well equipped and rank amongst the best in the kingdom. In addition to the ordinary school subjects the girls are taught cookery, laundry work, and housewifery and the boys receive instruction in hygiene, manual training and swimming.

There are three Secondary Schools :—
    Bede Collegiate School for Boys.
    Bede Collegiate School for Girls, and
    St. Anthony's Secondary School for Girls.

In addition to the above there are several Private Schools and a High School for Girls in the town. Sunderland Secondary Schools have a splendid reputation and the needs of all the various types of Secondary School pupils are provided for—whether such needs are quite general, or those of persons who mean to engage in Commercial life, Engineering or shipbuilding, or to enter the Medical, the Legal, the Teaching, or any other profession, or to go straight from school to the University.

The TECHNICAL COLLEGE provides courses of instruction in Engineering (Mechanical, Electrical, and Civil), Naval

Architecture, Mining, Mathematics, Chemistry, Physics, and Modern Languages. It is affiliated to Durham University and students of the College can obtain either the B.Sc., Degree in Engineering, or the Diploma of Associate of the College in Engineering upon passing the necessary examinations.

Sunderland has also an excellent system of Evening Schools, in connection with the local Technical College, for the teaching of Commercial and Technical subjects.

The SUNDERLAND SCHOOL OF ART occupies the top storey of the Town Hall, and is one of the most flourishing in England.

THE SUNDERLAND TRAINING COLLEGE for Teachers was opened on 22nd of September, 1908, for the training of schoolmasters and schoolmistresses. The temporary premises (Westfield House) are situated in Green Terrace, opposite the Technical College.

There is accommodation for 140 students. The principal of the college is Mr. S. Hoole, M.A.

TEACHERS WAR RECORD.

During the War of 1914 to 1918 the number of School masters who joined the Navy and Army was 23,145. Several Schoolmistresses volunteered as nurses and rendered splendid service in hospitals at home and in France.

Two hundred students and ex-students and two members of the staff from the local Training College were on active service as well as 77 schoolmasters from schools in Sunderland.

CASUALTIES AMONGST TEACHERS.

Two thousand one hundred teachers were killed or died from wounds. This included 37 connected with our Local Training College and the following nine local teachers :—

1. Arthur Coleman, St. Joseph's School.
2. Walter R. Goodrick, James Williams St. School.
3. Cecil Hands, Pallion School.
4. Charles L. Patterson, Pallion School.
5. J. A. Pinchen, Cowan Terrace „
6. James T. Robson, Stansfield St. „
7. Robert H. Stafford, Simpson St. „
8. Douglas Tweedie, Redby „
9. Fawcitt Wayman, Valley Road „

SUNDERLAND DAY TRAINING COLLEGE.
ROLL OF HONOUR.

Name.	Rank.	Regiment.	Killed.
Baker, Ward.	2nd Lt.	11th West Yorks.	Poperinghe.
Brock, Alf.	Capt.	6th D.L.I.	Hennial (Arras).
Cook, James	Pte.	7th D.L.I.	Ypres.
Chambers, N.	Pte.	22nd D.L.I.	Somme.
Dehn, Joseph	Pte.	7th D.L.I.	Died of illness.
Dobson, W. G.	Pte.	1/7 D.L.I.	Ypres.
Eggleston, A.	Sergt.	2/4 Lincoln Rgt.	St. Julien Rd.
Foley, John	Capt.	N.F. Ty'side Irish	Somme.
Foster, Chas.	Sergt.	D.L.I. & Leic. Rgt.	Zonnebeke.
Gibson, Mat.	Cpl.	7th D.L.I.	Ypres.
Goodrick, W.	Cpl. M.C.	7th D.L.I.	France.
Horn, John H.	2nd Lt.	L.N.L. Regt.	Halla, Cambrai.
Hodgson, John	2nd Lt.	7th D.L.I.	Italy.
Hauxwell, Geo.	Sergt.	1/7 D.L.I.	Ypres.
Hardy, George	Signalman	R.N.	Died at Sea.
Jones, R. A.	Major	Warwicks	France.
Lawson, James	Sergt.	22nd D.L.I.	Peronne.
Locke, Alex.	Pte.	7th D.L.I.	Ypres.
Monro, Duncan	Pte.	10th K.O.Y.L.I.	Ypres.
Mason, Ernest	Capt.	1/7 N. Fusiliers	Gooevaersvelde
MacNab, Alex.	Sergt.	27th N.F.	Somme.
Nasby, Frank	2nd Lt.	7th D.L.I.	Hargicourt.
Napier, J. C.	Pte.	7th D.L.I.	France.
Pattison, Chas.	Pte.	2/4 Leicester	Ypres.
Pattinson, T. E.	Cpl.	1/7 D.L.I.	Zonnebeke.
Rigg, Tyson	Sergt. M.M., K.C.	18th D.L.I.	Somme.
Rivers, Geo.	Pte.	18th D.L.I.	Hamel.
Richardson Alex.	Pte.	18th D.L.I.	Seclin.
Richardson, Wm.	Pte.	14th London Scot.	Hebuterne.
Rodda, John	L.-Cpl.	S.A. Scot. Inf.	France.
Robson, T.	Sergt.	6th D.L.I.	Poperinghe.
Rowell, J. F.	Gnr.	R.G.A.	France.
Stobbs, Henry	2nd Lt.	1/4 N.F.	Houthulst For'st
Sharp, A. G.	2nd Lt.	4th Border Regt.	France.
Sayer, Cecil O.	2nd Lt.	7th D.L.I.	Ypres.
Troughton, Wm.	L.-Cpl.	7th D.L.I.	Proven, Belgium
Warriner, T.A.L.	2nd Lt.	2/7 Worcester	Richebourge, St. Vaast.

"IN THIS WORLD THERE IS NO DEATH, BUT FORGETFULNESS."

The members of the National Union of Teachers established a War Aid Fund for Teachers, Soldiers, Sailors, Nurses, and their dependants, and the amount subscribed was £151,628. The Sunderland Teachers subscribed £1,056.

The Sunderland Parks   SUNDERLAND has four public parks which occupy 95 acres of ground. The oldest is the Mowbray Park, almost in the centre of the town, and consisting of the East and West Parks, opened in 1857, and the Extension Park opened in 1866 a total area of 23½ acres. This is one of the finest and most tastefully ornamented parks in the North of England.

It contains the Winter Gardens with its fine collection of tropical plants and ferns; a small pond with gold fish; a number of parrots and other birds in wire cages.

In the park, under a glass cupola, is a white marble statue commemorating a sad calamity at the Victoria Hall, in 1883, in which one hundred and eighty three children lost their lives. There are three bronze statues erected to the memory of Sunderland men; on the summit of Boyldon Hill stands that in memory of Major-General Sir Henry Havelock, K.C.B., whose services in the Indian Mutiny will never be forgotten. Close to this monument are two Russian guns, taken at Sebastopol in 1855 and presented by the Secretary of War to the town.

On a small knoll is the memorial to Jack Crawford, the Sunderland sailor who so gallantly nailed Admiral Duncan's flag to the mast of H.M.S. "Venerable" at the battle of Camperdown in 1797, when the Dutch were defeated.

The third statue is in memory of John Candlish, a Member of Parliament for the Borough from 1865 until his death in 1874. The park also has a small lake, a bowling green, tennis court, and bandstand. A very interesting feature of the Mowbray Park is Boyldon Hill, also known as Byldon, Bylding, and Building Hill. It is described in ancient records as "a certain close containing fourteen acres, or thereabouts, situated at the southeast part of, and within the township of Bishopwearmouth." Garbutt, writing in 1819, describes it as an eminence about a quarter of a mile to the south of Bishopwearmouth and says that it affords a great variety of interesting specimens of limestone. The hill has also been named the "Calton Hill of Sunderland."

It has always been a favourite spot for many of our townsfolk, for from the top may be obtained a grand view of the town and neighbourhood, the sea and the many ships in the offing. From time immemorial the inhabitants had liberty to dig and carry away stones from the hill for building, without any payment. A lime kiln was situated near the hill in ancient times. In 1779, when the notorious Paul Jones, the pirate, made his appearance at the mouth of the Wear, a beacon is said to have been lighted on the top of the hill; bonfires were also lighted on the same spot on Midsummer Eve in ancient times.

THE BURN PARK, the smallest of our parks, is divided into two parts by Durham Road. For centuries these six acres of ground, which form a pleasing scene with fine trees and well-kept flower beds, near to the heart of our town, were known as the Burn Fields. They were so named because of the Bishopwearmouth Burn which flowed through these fields. At one time, this land formed part of the common-lands, belonging to the inhabitants of Bishopwearmouth. Now-a-days many people pass through either part on their way to business; in the warm weather the Burn Parks are much appreciated by both young and old.

THE ROKER PARK, containing 32 acres, was opened in 1880. The land was given jointly by the late Sir Hedworth Williamson, Bart., and the Ecclesiastical Commissioners.

THE CLIFF PARK, which is near the sea, commands a fine view of the ocean, lighthouses and piers, and in the distance the pretty village of Whitburn. On the highest point a beautiful Anglican Cross stands, as a fitting memorial to perhaps our most famous son, the Venerable Bede. In this park there are also public bowling greens, tennis courts, and a bandstand, also a lake which is well patronised by owners of small sailing boats and model yachts. A handsome drinking fountain, erected in 1880 to commemorate the opening of the park, and also the Centenary of Sunday Schools, stands near the lake. The two figures of hay makers, which arouse much interest, for many years adorned the front of Squire Stafford's house.

Mr. Craven's Rope Works now occupy the site of the old house. A small "dene" extends through the Park to the sea-beach, where the largest of our coast caves, "Spotties's, or Monks' Hole," may be seen. The story runs that a foreign shipwrecked mariner took up his abode in this cave, and from the order of his garb, was nicknamed "Spottee," hence "Spottee's Hole." Tradition has it that this cave was the entrance to an underground passage to the Monastery of Monkwearmouth; it would thus be used by the Monks, and so became known as "Monks' Hole."

THE BARNES PARK, our latest addition to Sunderland Parks, is at the West End of the Borough, and is approached from Durham Road and Chester Road. The thirty-three acres forming the Barnes Park were purchased in 1904 for £8,500. During the depression of trade in 1907, it was decided to commence the laying out of the Park, in order to provide work for the unemployed. In addition to the practical gardeners, 2,798 men were employed with most satisfactory results. All the trees upon the land at the time of its acquisition, were allowed to remain, and a considerable number of oak, ash, beech and elm trees, as well as numerous shrubs and plants were added. Well made paths wind in and out in all directions, and at the West on the most elevated piece of ground, are two bowling greens, tennis courts, and a café. Barnes Park is situated in a beautiful little valley through which flows the Bishopwearmouth Burn, the water here forms a lake dotted with islands, the home of many water fowl. The surplus water forms a miniature water fall at the east end of the lake. In addition to a bandstand, an ancient cannon dredged from the River Wear is placed in a conspicuous position, so that our newest park is by no means the least interesting.

All our local birds visit the park in large numbers; there are also many birds of passage and winter visitors to be seen by the bird lover especially in the early morning. Nesting boxes are provided, and amongst the birds breeding regularly in the park may be mentioned the water hen, starlings, linnets, and grey birds. Snipe, water ousels, tits, diving ducks, and chaffinches may frequently be observed. During the summer months the beautiful roses, the fine shady trees, and pleasing stretches of well kept green, added to its natural picturesqueness, make this quite the most delightful of Sunderland Parks.

Roker   ROKER, the Brighton of Sunderland, is one of the most popular sea-side resorts of the North of England ; it is of easy access from the centre of the town and possesses all the attractions necessary for holidays makers. The broad stretch of sandy beach suitable for sea-bathing is a perfect spot for children of all ages ; two well built promenades (extending the whole length of the sea-front), give a fine view of the pier and lighthouse ; and visitors may watch the ships entering and leaving the port. The walk along the pier, which is half-a-mile long, is another attraction. Near to the beach is a very pretty park, which has been previously described. There are high limestone cliffs, honey-combed with caves, the best known being the Holey Rock, from which one views the new village of Seaburn and in the distance the pretty village of Whitburn. The climate is very bracing and thanks to the breezes from the North Sea, the heat is never oppressive. The inhabitants of Roker are fortunate in having the ever changing sea and the fresh countryside in close proximity.

CHAPTER XVII.

GREATER SUNDERLAND.

Just as we cannot understand a person thoroughly unless we know something of his home life and surroundings so we shall fail to grasp the real importance of Sunderland unless we know something of the district in which it lies. The County Borough of Sunderland, and the more or less closely connected and adjoining townships, villages, and rural districts, are often spoken of as "Greater Sunderland;" the total population being about 250,000.

SOUTHWICK, formerly a small village of great antiquity, one mile from Monkwearmouth, is now a very busy manufacturing district joined to Sunderland and noted for its shipbuilding yards, engineering works, and glass works. Southwick is included in the Parliamentary Borough, but possesses its own Urban District Council; there are four large elementary schools with accommodation for 4,000 pupils and the total population of this township is about 17,000.

CASTLETOWN, a new colliery village near Hylton Castle, is about one mile west of Southwick. It had formerly large iron works on the banks of the Wear, but these proving unsuccessful were closed down some years ago.

NORTH HYLTON, three and a half miles west of Sunderland, has a large shipbuilding yard and brick works. FORD or SOUTH HYLTON, on the opposite bank of the Wear, is noted for paper mills and cement works. From the village of North Hylton a pleasant footpath following the winding of the river leads to BIDDICK. This small village, quite a favourite calling place for boating parties from Sunderland, marks the western boundary of our port. In ancient times Biddick was said to have been inhabited by banditti, who set all authority at defiance; even in more recent times the officers of the excise were afraid of surveying the public houses unless they had protection; whilst the Press Gang only visited the place once and then had two of its members killed in a fray.

Behind the Inn stands the Worm Hill, round which tradition informs us "Ye Lambton Worme" curled itself nine times when it sought repose.

FULWELL, noted for its limestone quarries, is 1½ miles north of Sunderland. Twenty years ago it was a picturesque agricultural village, now it is a residential suburb of Sunderland joined to the town by the tramway system. Over 2,000 children in this district attend the two fine Council Schools provided by the Durham County Council. An ancient windmill occupies the hill to the west of the village, and from the hill there is a very fine view of Whitburn Bay and the adjoining coast line.

CLEADON, called in ancient times Clivedon, is a small village on the turnpike road between Sunderland and South Shields. In Boldon Book the Manor of Cleadon and Whitburn was occupied by 28 villeins and 12 cottagers. During Hatfield's Survey the district is described as having been temporarily abandoned owing to the devastations of the Scots.

WHITBURN, sometimes called the "Queen of Durham seaside villages" is 3 miles north of Sunderland. It is charmingly situated with a fine view of the beach and sea, the picturesque ancient church, and many fine residences, the chief being Whitburn Hall, erected in 1600, form a pleasing background to the quaint Fishermen's Cottages on the cliff banks. Five persons from Whitburn and four from Cleadon joined the rebellion of 1569, of whom two from each village were executed.

The parish of BOLDON is about 4 miles from Sunderland and has become of recent years a favourite residential district for local tradespeople. The ancient Manor of Boldon gave the title to "The Boldon Buke," as it was the first place mentioned in Bishop Pudsey's Survey of 1180. Boldon possesses a beautiful church of early English architecture, its peculiarly designed tower and spire being worthy of special mention.

OFFERTON or Higher Town, was one of the villages which Athelstan gave to the See of Durham as an appendage to that of Bishopwearmouth. Now-a-days Offerton is a small agricultural village ; in Saxon times an ancient monastic house existed in this village and it still possesses the remains of a fine old Jacobean manor house.

COX GREEN, a little riverside village on the Wear, noted for its golf course and freestone quarries, is also included in Greater Sunderland. The woods near to this little village, together with Penshaw Woods and Monument, have made it a favourite spot for picnic parties.

GRANGETOWN adjoins Sunderland on the south, trams running between the two places every few minutes. It is quite of recent growth and many of the inhabitants are engaged at the Hendon Paper Mills.

TUNSTALL township includes the Tunstall Hill which, towering 346 feet above the North Sea, forms the most important landmark in our immediate neighbourhood. A bare spot on the northern hill marks the place where for ages a bonfire has been built in times of rejoicing. The few dwellings which formed part of the ancient village of Tunstall are now practically joined to Silksworth.

SILKSWORTH Village and Silksworth Colliery are three miles south-west of Sunderland. The former, an ancient village, has several fine manors the chief being "Silksworth Hall" and "Silksworth House."

RYHOPE Village is pleasantly situated three and a-half miles south of our town, on the turnpike road leading to Stockton. It possesses a pretty Dene much frequented by children, and its colliery is one of the largest in the County.

OLD SEAHAM was included in Athelstan's gift to the patrimony of St. Cuthbert. The church retains traces of high antiquity including Saxon windows and other stone work.

SEAHAM HARBOUR a modern and rapidly increasing town of 16,000 inhabitants, owes its importance to its coal-mines, glass works, and harbour.

BURDON was formerly the most southern part of Bishopwearmouth parish ; it is now attached to the Easington Union. In Boldon Book the villages of East and West Burdon were known as Great and Little Burdon. Other places which may be included in Greater Sunderland are East, West, and Middle Herrington, and the village of Newbottle. These are chiefly agricultural villages, but there are several large collieries in close proximity.

Sunderland War Record WHEN the war broke out Sunderland became the centre of a large district, and 112,000 volunteers readily came forward prepared to go and fight the battle of Right against Might. Later on, when Lord Derby's Scheme came to the fore, no less than 90,000 men came to Sunderland and were enrolled, and later again large numbers of the manhood of the town and district entered the Army. In War Bonds Sunderland raised nearly £14,000,000, and something like £400,000 was invested in War Certificates. Large sums of money were also raised for the War Hospital and in connection with the V.A.D.'s and the King's Fund. This all shows that Sunderland people are determined to uphold the flag of the British Empire.

(Extract from the Mayor's speech at a public meeting held in the Town Hall, on 11th February, 1919).

EVENTS OF LOCAL INTEREST.

1716. Hospital established in Church Street, by the Freemen of Sunderland. The building was demolished when the Rectory was built.
1740. First Sunderland Workhouse erected in Church Walk.
1750. Seamen's Hall erected in Assembly Garth.
1786. Local Sunday Schools first established.
1787. First Bank established in the town.
1795. Subscription Library commenced.
1795. The Barracks opened.
1814. The Exchange in High Street opened. (It is now used as a Seamen's Mission).
1824. Sunderland first lighted with gas.
1833. First hackney coach in town.
1836. Sunderland and Durham railway opened.
1837. Borough Police established.
1839. Sunderland and South Shields railway opened.
1839. Foundation stone of Athenæum laid by H.R.H. The Duke of Sussex.
1842. Police Court in West Wear Street opened.
1847. Sunderland and South Shields Water Company established.
1852. The first local emigrant ship the Lizzie "Webber," left the Wear for Australia.
1860. The 3rd V.B. Durham Light Infantry, and 1st Durham Artillery Volunteers were enrolled. In 1908 both corps were absorbed in the new Territorial Army.
1863. Visit of Channel Fleet. Other visits in 1874, 1895, and 1903.
1879. Central Railway Station opened.

1879. Horse Trams commenced. Electric Trams in 1900.
1890. The New Town Hall, Fawcett Street, opened. The first Town Hall was situated in Assembly Garth. The second in Exchange Buildings, High Street East and the third in West Wear Street.
1907. The first Court of Quarter Sessions held.
1910. Sunderland Labour Exchange installed in the Old Custom House, High Street East.
1918. 11th Dec., Polling Day, 28th Dec., Declaration of Polling. Sir Hamar Greenwood and Mr. R. M. Hudson elected.

INDEX

A
'Achilles'	130
'Amity'	131
Art Gallery	174–5
Athelstan	36
Austin, S. P. & Sons	133

B
Ballast Hills	104–5
Barnes Park	189
Bartram R. A. & Sons	134
Batteries	85–6
Bede	29–30
Bede	161
Bede Memorial Cross	32–33
Benedict Biscop	26–28
Benedict Biscop	160
Biddick	191
Bishop Auckland	124
Bishopwearmouth Church	36
Bishopwearmouth Church (illus)	opp. 38
Bishopwearmouth Grange (illus)	opp. 122
Bishopwearmouth Rectory	64–5
Bishopwearmouth Rectory (illus)	opp. 53
'Blackbird'	130
Blind Institute	179
Blumer, John & Co.	136
Boldon	193
Boldon Book	46
Bowling	117–8
Bridge—Queen Alexandra	82–3
Bridge—Railway	82
Bridge—Sunderland	80
Bridge End Pottery	147
Bronze Age	3–5
'Bucephalus'	130
Bull-baiting	114–5
Burdon	194
Burn Park	187–8

C
Cage	120–1
Castletown	191
Celtic Age	5–6
Charter—Bishop Morton	54–57
Charter—Bishop Pudsey	43–46
Charter—Henry III	48
Children's Hospital	179
'Chowringhee'	131
Church—Bishopwearmouth	36
Church—Sunderland Parish	83–4
Civil War	57–64
Clanny, Dr.	165
Clark, George Ltd.	157
Cleadon	192
Cliff Park	188
Cloy Day	108–10
Coal Trade	139–141
Cock Fighting	112–114
Colliers	142
Commission of 1558	53
Concord	129–30
'Coppenami'	132
Cox Green	193
Crawford, Jack	163
Crowley, Sir Ambrose	68
Crown, J. & Sons	136

D
Danish Invasions 33–36
Deptford Pottery 148
District Nursing
  Association 181
Docks 74–5
Donnison, Elizabeth 168
Doxford, William &
  Sons 134–5
Duncan Dunbar 131

E
Eastgate 123
Education 182–6
Emery, John 166
Events List 195
Eye Infirmary 178

F
Fairley, Sarah 169
Fishing—Salmon 159
Fishing—Whale 158
Ford Paper Works 158
Ford Pottery 147
Forts & Batteries 85–6
Foxhunting 115
Frosterley 124
Fulwell 192
Furriers 159

G
Garrison Pottery 146
Gibson, Jane 168
Glass Trade 152–6
Goodchild, Lawrence 166
Grange, the (illus) opp. 122
Grange School 182–3
Grangetown 193
Green, John 166
Grindstones 160

H
Hartley, James 153–4
Havelock, Charles F. 161
Havelock, Sir Henry 161
Havelock Thomas 161–2
Havelock, William 161
Havelock-Alan,
  Sir Henry 162
Hendon 93–4
Hendon Dene 96–7
Hendon Old Mill 94–5
Hendon Paper Works 157–8
High Southwick
  Pottery 148
High Street 91–92
Hilton family 41–43
Hodgson, Joseph R. 163–4
Hornsby, Captain 163
Horseracing 117
Hudson, Charity 181
Hylton Castle in
  1746 (illus) opp. 106
Hylton, N. 191
Hylton, S. 191

I
Ireshope Village 122
Iron bridge (illus) opp. 98
Iron ships 131
Iron trade 159

K
Keels and Keelmen 143–5

L
Laing and Sons 132–3
Library 172
Lifeboats 76–80
Lighthouse, Roker 73
Lime Trade 158
'Lord Duncan' 130

M
Maling, George 166–7

Marine Engines	156–7	Police Station	176
Market	100–101	Population and growth	88–90
Meadley, George Wilson	166	Potteries	145
Monkwearmouth Church prior to 1874 (illus)	opp. 25	Pottery, Roman	145–6
		Prehistoric pottery	8–9
		Prehistoric remains	9–16
Monkwearmouth Estates	65	Prehistoric stone circles	6–7
Monkwearmouth Hospital	181	Prehistoric times	1
		Priestman, John & Co.	138
Morton, Bishop	54–57	Public Library	172
Mowbray Park	186	Pudsey Bishop charter	43–46
Museum	173		

N

Neolithic Age	2–3	**Q**	
Norman Invasion	38–41	Queen Alexandra bridge	82–3
North Hylton Potteries	146	**R**	
		Rackley, Cpt. Stephen	165
O		Railway Bridge	82
Offerton	193	Richardson Westgarth & Co.	157
Orphan Asylum	180–1		
Osbourne, Graham & Sons	136–7	Richmond St. Pottery	147
		Riding the Stang	118–20
		River Wear Commissioners	70
P			
Palaeolithic Age	1–2	Robinson, Edward	160
Paper making	157–8	Roker	190
Parish Church	83–4	Roker Lighthouse	73–4
Perambulating the Boundaries	106–8	Roker Park	188
		Roker Pier	73
Pickersgill, William & Sons	135	Roman altars	21–2
		Roman period	16–19
Pier of 1669	67–8	Roman pottery	145–6
Piers, Lighthouses and Docks	70	Roman remains	19–21
		Roxby, Sam	166
Pile, William	131	Royal Infirmary	177–8
Pillory	121–2	Royal Institute for the Blind	179
Plantagenet Sunderland	50–52		

Ryhope 193

S
Saint Crispin's Day 108
St. Michael's Church 36
Salmon fishing 159
Salt 160
Seaham 194
Sheepfold Pottery 147
Shipbuilding 128–39
Short Bros 136
Silksworth 193
South Hylton Pottery 147
Southwick 191
Southwick Pottery 147
Spa Well 86
Spottie's Hole 188
Stanfield, Clarkson 167
Stang riding 118–20
Stanhope 123–4
Stocks 120
Street names 90
Sunderland bridge 80–82
Sunderland church
 (illus) opp. 70
Sunderland docks 74–5
Sunderland Parish
 Church 83–4
Sunderland pottery 146
Sunderland
 Shipbuilding Co. 137
Swan Hunter &
 Wigham Richardson 138

T
Taylor, Tom 160
Technical College 175–6
Technical College 183–4

Thompson, J. L. &
 Sons 135
Thompson, Robert
 & Sons 133–4
Town Hall 171–2
Town Moor 84–5
Training College 184–6
Travel 103–4
Tunstall 193

U
'Undaunted' 131

V
Victoria Hall 175

W
Walcher, Bishop 39
War Record 194
Warden Law 10–11
Water Supply 101–3
Watts, Harry 164–5
Wear 122–7
Wear Concrete
 Shipbuilding Co. 138–9
Wear Glass Works 153–5
Wear Potteries 147
Wearhead 122
Wearmouth Panns 53
Wearmouth Walk 92–3
Well 86
Westgate 123
Whale fishing 158
Whitburn 192
Williamson, Dame
 Dorothy 168
Witton-le-Wear 124
Wolsingham 124
Woodcock, Mrs. 168